IN PURSUIT OF A NOBLE CAUSE

To David,

Thank you for supporting me and my book.

I wish you continued success and many blessings.

Sincerely,

Arturo

12·19·23

IN PURSUIT OF A NOBLE CAUSE

A SOCIAL JUSTICE LEADERSHIP JOURNEY

ARTURO A. NORIEGA

MANUSCRIPTS
PRESS

IN PURSUIT OF A NOBLE CAUSE
A Social Justice Leadership Journey

ISBN
979-8-88926-782-9   *Paperback*
979-8-88926-783-6   *Ebook*

To my family and the Centro team:

I love you! Without you, I would not have become my best self.

And survived to tell the stories in this book.

CONTENTS

————◆————

FOREWORD

———◆◇◆———

Reflecting on my journey as an immigrant woman, entrepreneur, and mother, I am filled with immense gratitude for the opportunities and support that have shaped my life.

With great pleasure and excitement, I introduce you to this remarkable book, *In Pursuit of a Noble Cause*, authored by a man whose dedication and expertise have transformed the lives of countless individuals like me—Arturo Noriega.

My name is Adela Orucuta de Arellano, and I hail from Mexico City. When I arrived in the United States with my family, full of dreams and aspirations, we faced the harsh reality of significant financial hardships. It was a daunting experience, arriving in a new country without a dollar to our name. But my determination to improve the lives of my family and contribute to the community propelled me forward, urging me to establish a daycare business in El Cerrito, California. This business would nurture and care for children while providing for my loved ones.

However, I soon discovered that starting a business in a foreign land challenged me. Denied credit due to a lack of financial education, language barriers, and a dearth of knowledge about advocating for my dreams, I was disheartened and helpless. At this critical juncture in my entrepreneurial journey, I was introduced to Arturo Noriega—an extraordinary guide who would change the trajectory of my life forever.

In February 2009, I was assigned Arturo as my coach through Creating Economic Opportunities for Women, an organization teaching me how to start a small business while teaching us English as a Second Language. From the moment we met, Arturo's genuine, humble, and compassionate nature shone through, instilling a sense of hope and possibility within me. With his unwavering support and deep understanding of the challenges faced by individuals like me, Arturo became a beacon of light on my path to success.

Throughout my entrepreneurial journey, Arturo's expertise and mentorship were invaluable. His strategic management acumen, honed over twenty years of experience, and his profound insights into leadership development have filled the gaps that once hindered my business aspirations. Through his guidance, I became the basis of why Centro Community Partners, an organization founded by Arturo, was formed—a testament to his unwavering commitment to helping others overcome obstacles and achieve their dreams.

In Pursuit of a Noble Cause is a book that embodies Arturo Noriega's dedication to empowering individuals on their social entrepreneurship journeys. Packed with crucial insights, practical advice, and real-life examples, this book is an indispensable roadmap, guiding readers through the complexities of starting and growing a social impact organization. It equips aspiring entrepreneurs with the tools to overcome obstacles, stay focused, and achieve their goals.

Arturo's motivation to delve deep into social entrepreneurship stems from his personal experiences as the child of immigrant parents from Peru. He intimately understands the needs and struggles of individuals starting in a new country. His empathy and insight form the bedrock of this book, offering readers the inspiration and guidance required to navigate economic development systems, fill gaps, and overcome prejudices that prevent individuals like me from accessing crucial resources such as entrepreneurship education, financial literacy, credit, and microloans.

My journey as an entrepreneur gives me immense satisfaction and joy. Despite the countless obstacles I encountered, with Arturo and Centro's help, I established my business–World of the Children Daycare. This venture provided for my family and allowed me to make a meaningful contribution to the community. Witnessing the positive outcomes that have emerged from my struggles has reinforced my belief in the power of perseverance and sacrifice.

As you embark on your entrepreneurial journey, I implore you to embrace the wisdom shared within the pages of this book. Arturo's vision of more equitable socioeconomic systems, commitment to leadership development, and genuine desire to empower individuals from underserved communities make him the ideal author for this transformative guide. By believing in yourself, assessing your abilities, and embracing shared values, you will gain the confidence and resources necessary to succeed.

Remember, entrepreneurship is not solely about amassing wealth but serving your customers and making a lasting impact. Cultivate a habit of continuous learning, explore the resources offered by Centro Community Partners, and utilize this book as a powerful tool to fuel your motivation and determination. Never lose sight of your goals, and remember that you can succeed.

I sincerely hope my story gives you a glimpse of the remarkable journey that Arturo and Centro Community Partners can help you embark upon. Like me, you can achieve your dreams, overcome obstacles, and create a better future. Let the guidance within these pages empower you to transform your aspirations into reality. May your journey be filled with resilience, growth, and the unwavering pursuit of a noble cause.

Adela Orucuta de Arellano
Immigrant, Entrepreneur, and Proud Mother

INTRODUCTION

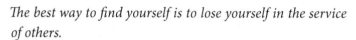

The best way to find yourself is to lose yourself in the service of others.

—MAHATMA GANDHI

In the depths of despair, I found myself in a dimly lit room in Pacifica, California, gazing into the vast darkness that mirrored my emptiness. The crashing waves at Rockaway Beach seemed to echo the turmoil in my soul.

The weight of the devastating news hit me like a punch to the gut. The 2008 financial crisis claimed my job, leaving me feeling lost and broken. *Why me?* I questioned, grappling with self-doubt and a sense of inadequacy. Despite my hard work, recognition, and sacrifices, I was deemed expendable, a casualty of a ruthless corporate world. The room swallowed me whole as I spiraled into darkness, desperately crying out for guidance. I started to pray.

I was immersed in a world of vibrant colors and exotic flavors in India just months earlier. Bangalore's smoky air carried the scent of burning wood fires while the bustling cityscape unfolded before my eyes. I convinced myself I was content as a management consultant, relishing the trappings of success. Yet, deep down, I was merely fooling myself.

My job devoured my time and consumed my spirit, leaving little room for anything else. I was being led by bosses who relished pursuing wealth and power. These values are typical of capitalistic systems and work fine for most people. However, I sought to be a part of a genuine effort to the community's economic development and make a positive and meaningful impact.

Day by day, a part of me withered away, unnoticed by those around me, including myself. I sought solace in food, succumbing to an unhealthy cycle of overeating that further fueled my discontent. The toll on my physical and mental well-being was undeniable, and the price I paid was a detachment from the joys of life—missed birthdays, graduations, and cherished moments with loved ones.

It felt like I failed in every aspect of my existence—my health, relationships, career, and more. The notion that a career in consulting and finance were the paths for me was ingrained in my mind, but they only led me down a path of unhappiness, loneliness, and illness. Amidst the despair, I held onto the silver linings. The professional training and world travel shaped my skills and provided a foundation for what lay ahead.

Yet, there was an even darker layer to my struggles, a reality I couldn't ignore. I faced discrimination as a person of color in a predominantly White industry. Unequal pay, limited opportunities, and the constant reminder that I was seen as less than my White counterparts — a painful truth permeated the consulting and finance world. I was belittled, questioned, and felt inferior simply because of my skin color.

I became a lost soul, unrecognizable even to myself. At the age of forty, I hit rock bottom. But little did I know that this moment of despair would ignite a fire within me, propelling me on a path of redemption, resilience, and the pursuit of social justice.

Navigating Childhood with Learning Disabilities

Growing up in Santa Clara, California, during the 1970s and '80s was stepping into a vibrant tapestry of nature and diverse cultures. The landscape was adorned with sprawling fruit orchards and cornfields, nourished by the months of continuous rainfall that transformed everything into a lush, green paradise. In those simpler times, drive-in movie shows entertained us, and the streets were safe havens for kids to explore on their bikes. As a child, nothing was quite like the exhilaration of riding through the muddy trails of the orchards or alongside the meandering creeks.

Nestled within a low-to-moderate-income immigrant community, my home reflected the rich multicultural and multiethnic experiences. On my street alone, one could encounter the vibrant cultures of China, Ghana, Germany, Portugal, India, Korea, Mexico, Ireland, Italy, and, of course, my heritage, Peru. Each step would immerse me in a symphony of languages while the enticing aromas of diverse home cuisines wafted through the air every evening. It was a place where children played together, switching effortlessly between languages, before returning to their respective cultural havens.

Being the youngest of nine children and the only one born in the United States, my family history echoes Lima, Peru. My mother, Olga, was indigenous, and my father, Oscar, was mestizo (a person of mixed blood). I proudly inherited my mother's striking features—dark brown skin and flowing, wavy black hair. While our family was a beautiful blend of races, I found a deep connection to my Peruvian indigenous roots, growing up primarily speaking Spanish within the nurturing embrace of our home.

But life had a surprise for me—dyslexia, a condition that ran in my family and shaped my journey unexpectedly. Growing up with dyslexia proved challenging, as reading became a formidable hurdle. While other children effortlessly read, I found solace in problem-solving and hands-on exploration. Recognizing my struggle, I worked with a speech therapist. During this time, I realized my mind worked differently and possessed unique strengths waiting to be unveiled. However, I was deeply embarrassed and ashamed about my reading disability, prompting me to conceal it from others. I became a master of ingenious strategies to complete reading assignments, constantly finding creative ways to stay afloat academically. In fifth grade, I devised covert operations, "borrowing" reading materials not meant to leave the classroom. Under cover of night, I read the pages painstakingly slowly, but I remembered everything I read. Luckily, I returned them to their rightful place before anyone noticed. My secret missions empowered me, ensuring I would not fall behind again.

Little did I know that this was the first of many challenges I would covertly navigate to reclaim my power.

Sowing Seeds of Social Justice

My parents worked as cleaners to make ends meet, but deep down, they aspired to be entrepreneurs. Sadly, discriminatory practices in accessing capital stood as formidable barriers, preventing them from realizing their dreams of business ownership. I was merely seven years old when I witnessed my father's hopeful attempt to secure a small business loan, only to face a resounding denial. Memories of their disappointment remain etched in my mind to this day. In Lima, Peru, my parents met while working in my father's family business, a thriving enterprise specializing in leather products. Eager to replicate their business in the United States, my father's entrepreneurial dreams were halted by being denied that crucial loan. Instead, he toiled away for over three decades, holding two jobs as a janitor at IBM and PG&E. My mother, Olga, was a house cleaner before becoming a team leader in Intel's microprocessors clean room. While my parents possessed remarkable talent, my mother's natural gifts as a singer, community organizer, and leader shone brightly.

In the 1970s, my brothers Oscar and Domingo joined the United Farm Workers (UFW) movement, taking a stand against the unfair treatment of farm workers in California. They marched alongside Cesar Chavez, raising public awareness and advocating for improved working conditions, fair wages, and the right to unionize. Motivated by a quest for social justice, they embraced nonviolent protests, igniting my earliest memories of witnessing the struggle for worker rights and equality on our black-and-white television during the evening news. My mother was furious with them for being jailed and missing class at Santa Clara University. She didn't want them to get involved with politics and get killed by the police. My brothers highlighted the immense importance of their fight for justice when they came home to visit.

Unbeknownst to me, my childhood abruptly came to an end. At fourteen, my world shattered when my mother was diagnosed with cancer. By the time I turned sixteen, she had passed away, leaving an irreparable void in my heart. Overnight, my world crumbled, and our once-unified family fell into disarray. I became trapped in a nightmare, unable to awaken from the heart-wrenching reality. Our beloved Olga, only fifty-six years old, passed away within the confines of our home, leaving behind a void that could not be filled. For three agonizing years, I grappled with immense anger, mourning the loss of the guiding force in our lives. Our once close-knit family was fractured, unable to come together without engaging in hurtful conflicts fueled by the trauma we collectively endured.

The experiences of witnessing my parents' struggle to start their own business, our family's journey of immigration fraught with mistreatment and discrimination, and my brothers' unwavering dedication to fighting for the human rights of others propelled me onto a path of transformation and change. The intertwined forces of pain and social justice have emerged as powerful catalysts for me to drive meaningful impact. The seeds of social transformation took root within the depths of my soul and the quest for a fairer society.

A Divided Economic Development System

At different points in my educational, professional, and personal life experiences, I confronted many types of racism, including individual, interpersonal, institutional, systemic, and structural—not to mention disability discrimination and bias. But it didn't matter. My keen awareness of the socioeconomic systems that created these challenges for people of color helped to shape me and initiated a journey to change systems. I needed to act. It took me a little longer to gain the confidence to nurture the power and insight to make the changes I wanted to see in the world.

The following table explains the different types of racism:

Term	Definition	Examples
Individual Racism	Personal beliefs and attitudes toward other races that affect the way a person treats people of color.	A person believing in White supremacy, telling or laughing at a racist joke, sharing a racist post on social media.
Interpersonal Racism	Treating others with discriminatory behavior that ranges from microaggressions to physical violence.	A person using slurs or showing aggression toward people of color, mistreating others based on their skin color.
Institutional Racism	Policies or behaviors within an organization intended to discriminate against people of color.	A hiring manager disqualifies candidates based on their names, citing a "cultural fit" that's actually discriminatory.
Systemic Racism	Perpetuated discrimination within a system that was founded on racist principles or practices.	A social work department lacks diversity among staff and students, despite training them to service communities of color.
Structural Racism	Cultural values in a society are so ingrained in daily life that they are seen as "the way things are."	A judge gives a lengthier sentence to a person of color than a White person with the same charges.

Source: (University of Southern California 2021).

After more than twenty years of working in economic development systems, it is clear we need innovation, social justice, and racial equity to be a part of the foundation of these systems. This is precisely why I started a nonprofit. My team and I develop and lead the socioeconomic change that promotes access to equitable systems. After seeing low-income women entrepreneurs of color being denied access to capital from the financial system that doesn't want to give to them because of their gender, color, or socioeconomic status, we need to work toward social justice.

The challenges of the small business economic development infrastructure, such as discrimination and systemic racism in financial institutions that create barriers to accessing capital, must be addressed. Outdated US Small Business Administration census data hinder appropriate policy decisions and a deeper understanding of micro- and small-business needs. The lack of timely information affects private and government investment into the system that helps to create small- and microenterprises, highlighting the importance of a well-functioning ecosystem for entrepreneurial development. The current US model focuses on individual entrepreneurs rather than a collaborative ecosystem that provides support services, including capital. This creates a problem as entrepreneurs often need to seek business resources from different sources, causing ecosystem and infrastructure inefficiencies and a lack of access.

My nonprofit leadership experience taught me to prioritize the organization's mission, vision, and shared values to focus the team's efforts on maximizing community impact and innovation. My background as a child of immigrants from

Peru fostered a strong connection with immigrant communities and a drive to support them. My international experience shaped my global perspective, professional acumen, and leadership style, emphasizing the importance of learning from mistakes and failures with grace and humility.

The Big Picture

Inspired by helping others launch their small businesses, in 2010, I founded a nonprofit called Centro Community Partners (Centro), which provides entrepreneurship education, financial literacy access to capital, and coaching to low-to-moderate-income women entrepreneurs. Centro's social justice work aims to bridge the racial wealth gap and empower underserved communities by supporting micro- and small-business development.

My vision is to create a comprehensive economic development system that combines a collaborative ecosystem, technology innovation, asset-building resources, and education to close the racial wealth gap. I propose a socioeconomic community-based solution that offers equitable access to a national virtual hub of entrepreneurship resources for low-to-moderate-income entrepreneurs in underserved communities.

Centro's mission is to serve underserved communities, including women, immigrants, Black, and indigenous people of color (BIPOC), by helping them build small businesses for economic empowerment. While Centro has successfully developed programs to assist low-income entrepreneurs, its future focus is completing building a social justice-oriented economic development system that not only fills in the gaps but allows entrepreneurs to achieve financial stability and create economic mobility for their families.

To achieve a more equitable society, tackling discrimination and unconscious bias within the investment community is necessary. Promoting inclusivity and diversity in financial institutions ensures equal access to investment opportunities and resources for people of color. Additionally, addressing the need for access to essential factors like financial literacy, business planning, and entrepreneurship education is crucial. By providing culturally relevant and accessible financial education, individuals from marginalized communities can make informed financial decisions and participate in wealth-building activities. While achieving structural transformation takes time, addressing these obstacles will help close the racial wealth gap and create a more equitable society.

My priority is to foster community-uniting and rebuilding systems for those discriminated against for their color, gender, and disabilities. I aim to serve and contribute to the transformative process of entrepreneurs and social impact leaders who want to realize their dreams of a better life for themselves, their families, and their community.

We can create better systems for inclusive economic systems and establish lasting enterprises led by people of color that result from their creative force and labor of love. People should be able to retire with dignity and financial freedom and leave generational wealth to their descendants. That would make our ancestors happy.

In the following pages, I share personal experiences, insights, and lessons that led me to become a leader and found an innovative social impact organization. You will find ideas and practical approaches to help change agents, students of leadership, and mission-driven professionals who serve their communities.

I outline the path and the systems we developed that can revolutionize an industry. In this book, I share our story.

CHAPTER 1

EQUITY FOR ALL

———◆◇◆———

Injustice anywhere is a threat to justice everywhere.
—DR. MARTIN LUTHER KING, JR.

Injustice as the Driver of Purpose

What would the world look like if people of color could grow their power? The power to have self-determination and thrive without the barriers of interpersonal, institutional, systemic, and structural racism. Could we see the light at the end of the racial equity tunnel? Is it possible to create such a world in our lifetime? This new world would change everything for people of color and create equality for all. Can it be achieved through peaceful methods?

I'm tired of living in fear because of my skin color. I'm of mixed races—White and native Peruvian indigenous, giving me dark brown skin and black hair. Recently, I remembered one morning I walked a couple of blocks from home in my neighborhood in Rockaway Beach in Pacifica, California, after having breakfast. The sky was blue, and I could hear the sound of the waves crashing on the beach. I was excited because I was packed and ready to fly to Peru that day to visit my family when I heard a voice from afar call for me. As I looked over, it was a Pacifica police officer. I was unsure what to think; I was surprised he called me, but I walked over to him without issue. I had to cross the street to do so. I cautiously looked both ways for traffic and walked over to the police officer.

His name was Officer Smith, and he asked me why I was in the neighborhood in a doubting tone. Looking at him without emotion, I quickly said, "I have lived here for over twenty years." My answer irritated him, and he retorted, "Prove it!" At that point, Officer Smith put his hand on his gun. I realized he was harassing and intimidating me. I began to fear for my life.

As cool-headed as I could muster, I said, "Sure, let me show you my identification." My heart pounded in my chest. He took my ID and asked me to wait as he checked the police computer in his car. All the terrifying police confrontations I had heard about raced through my mind. When he returned, he said, "I am writing you a ticket for jaywalking across the street." I said, "But you asked me to come to you." He said nothing and wrote me a ticket for $200 for crossing the street. He grinned when he handed me the ticket and said, "Maybe you should think twice about living here. Have a nice day!" The ugly face of racism and discrimination showed itself once again. I was powerless, frightened, and demoralized, but I walked away with my life. It was a good day!

Have you experienced injustices, discrimination, or racism or seen it happen to others? Racial discrimination occurs to all people of color regardless of their socioeconomic background. I have seen it happen to the rich and poor in more than the thirty countries I have visited in Asia, Africa, Europe, Latin America, and North America. After forty years, I got tired of experiencing these injustices in the systems we rely on to keep us employed, safe, healthy, and sheltered. Systemic racism is everywhere, unfortunately, but if we work together, we can build better racial justice systems. Diverse and inclusive systems allow the community to achieve real prosperity. My experiences with racism have fueled my desire to become steadfast and focused on my purpose—to create more social justice and racial equity-based systems in our community. Where to start to dismantle these old systems of hate?

Let us define what we mean by racial equity and social justice. According to the Annie E. Casey Foundation, *"Racial justice is the systematic fair treatment of people of all races that results in equitable opportunities and outcomes for everyone. All people can achieve their full potential, regardless of race, ethnicity, or the community in which they live"* (The Annie E. Casey Foundation 2020). Social justice means equal rights and equitable opportunities for all (San Diego Foundation 2022).

Keep in mind that equality and equity are not synonyms. Equality means that each individual or group of people is given the same resources or opportunities. Equity recognizes everyone has different life circumstances and allocates the resources and opportunities needed for an equal outcome (Marin Health and Human Services 2021).

These definitions provide a point of reference to examine how racial equity and social justice can be embedded in the critical systems that form the foundation of the US economy—entrepreneurship. According to Costa, entrepreneurship is the state of being an entrepreneur or a person who organizes, manages, and assumes the risk of a business with the goal of generating economic value. The term is derived from the Old French verb *entreprendre*, "to undertake" (Costa 2022).

Why entrepreneurship? Because our story begins there.

Adela's Entrepreneurship Story

On one chilly February afternoon in 2009, I made my way to Creating Economic Opportunity for Women (CEO Women) in Oakland, California, for my first day as a volunteer. CEO Women was a nonprofit microenterprise development organization providing entrepreneurship training and teaching immigrant women English as a Second Language. In one of Oakland's older downtown buildings, I met Adela. We smiled at each other during our first meeting as we were introduced. We were both excited and nervous. Adela was well-dressed in a suit jacket and was a petite Latina woman with a warm smile. I was assigned as her volunteer business advisor for a few months. During our first meeting, we got a chance to get to know each other. She told me about being an immigrant from Mexico City, her husband, and her children and how they lived in Berkeley. She shared how she loved attending the entrepreneurship courses at CEO Women. We talked about our families, and I shared about my parents immigrating from Peru. I told her why I wanted to help as a volunteer advisor and that I was assigned to work with her.

Adela's big dream was to own her own business. She wanted to have a children's daycare service. Adela would light up when she talked about her business idea and how she envisioned it. She was talking so fast that I had trouble keeping up with writing my notes. I remember how much I admired her confidence and feisty character, partly because she knew exactly what she needed to get her business off the ground and partly because she was a visionary. I could see that Adela clearly saw her child daycare service business in her mind. She dictated all the details to me. She already knew what type of house would be needed, the toys she would have for the children, the layout of the activity rooms, and even the color schemes to make learning fun. She knew that she wanted to grow from daycare into a preschool. As we sat down during our first meeting, I listened to her with great interest and curiosity.

By the end of our first meeting, Adela said, "I've had this dream for so long, Arturo. Would you help me?" At that very moment, I was reminded of my parents asking for help. I flashed to when I was a little boy, and my parents wanted to start their small business. I remember my parents were entrepreneurs in Peru but wanted their own leather apparel products store. They met as employees in a small leather factory in Peru. They were denied credit for the working capital to start their small business, ending their dreams of business ownership in the US. Even though they had good credit and owned their house and cars, I had forgotten that sad story.

I snapped back to the moment with Adela, and I responded to her, "*Claro que si!* (Of course), I will, *comenzamos ya!*

(Let's get started now!)" Adela's face lit up again, and she hugged me tightly.

My eyes began welling with tears, and I connected deeply with Adela. I was led to this special moment. Could it be destiny? I could feel myself connecting with Adela on a spiritual level. I did not understand it, but it felt right, and I committed myself to helping her start her daycare business. At that moment, I was happy and fulfilled for the first time in a very long time. I felt useful and valued and knew deeply that I could help her reach her dream. I remember walking out of the building from our first meeting and crying from the joy of having the experience with Adela. I started to feel the healing power of serving others.

As we worked on her business idea, we would draft her business plan, work out the business model, create her financial projections, and estimate her startup costs. I thought her idea was sound, but she needed to overcome fundamental challenges, such as moving her family from her one-bedroom apartment to a house that could function as her daycare center. Nevertheless, Adela had an advantage in that she was already licensed in California to care for infants and toddlers. She was ready for the next step.

We worked together for four months to complete her plan and financial projections. We estimated her startup costs to be about $10,000 to get her business and equipment approved, certified, and time pressed heavily on her. Adela was anxious to start her business because her husband lost hours at his job at a steel factory in Berkeley due to the financial crisis affecting the economy.

Once her business plan and financials were completed, I searched for the $10,000 in capital she needed to start her business. I helped Adela apply to several commercial banks and nonprofit Community Development Financial Institutions (CDFIs). The CDFI system comprises nonprofit banks, credit unions, loan funds, microloan funds, and venture capital providers with the mission to foster economic development and revitalize low-income neighborhoods and underserved people of color. They needed to fill in the credit gap created by commercial banks.

We waited for the responses, but unfortunately, all the financial institutions denied her the microloan she needed. They repeatedly stated, *"Adela did not have any credit history."* Adela's dream of starting her business would slip away. She was defeated and depressed. She could not understand why this happened to her since she paid all her bills and rent on time. When we talked about the denial of the microloan, she cried and talked about how important this business was for her family to become financially stable. She was left out in the cold and ignored by the financial system.

I tried to reassure Adela that we would raise money through other means, but I admitted to her that I did not know where it would come from. The initial funding stage is the most challenging stage for new businesses to overcome because the business is just an idea and needs proving. It is more difficult if you come from underserved low-income communities or a person of color because discrimination causes a lack of access to startup capital. I asked Adela if she could ask friends or family for seed capital to invest in her. She told me her friends did not have extra money to invest and were barely making ends meet.

It was August 2009, and Adela called me to say she could not wait any longer. She was desperate and thought of selling her car to start her business. She began to cry on the phone about how her husband got his hours cut, and they struggled to pay the rent. After that call, I was so upset and frustrated! I asked myself, *How can I help her? Why won't the CDFIs help her?* Adela's situation reminded me again of my parents' experiences of discrimination when they wanted to start a small business. They were also denied access to capital. What is it about the US economic development system that keeps entrepreneurs like Adela from accessing capital and realizing their business dreams?

I could not stop thinking about how the nonprofit CDFIs were not helpful. Why? Since the US government created them to help underserved communities, why did they act more like commercial banks instead of community capital resources bridging the financial needs of the low-income women entrepreneurs of color they were meant to serve? I started to look deeper into the issue and researched why Adela was denied access to capital. What I found shocked me. It was not just happening to Adela. It affected millions of microenterprises throughout the US.

In 2009, about 25 million microenterprises existed in the US, and about 10.8 million had trouble accessing bank financing (Klein and Wayman 2008). Microenterprises are businesses with less than five employees. The lack of access to capital was systemic and a market failure fact.

Adela's case is intriguing because she diligently followed all the steps in her entrepreneurial journey. She enrolled in the CEO Women's introductory entrepreneurship training course to gain financial literacy and understand the fundamentals of enterprise development. She collaborated with a seasoned business advisor to develop a comprehensive business plan, and her idea showed promise with projected profitability within two years. Adela even saved 20 percent of her capital, as required for the microloan application. She fulfilled all the requirements on paper to secure the necessary funding.

However, despite her unwavering efforts, Adela faced a disheartening setback when her microloan application was rejected due to a lack of credit history. What remains hidden in the financial institutions' shadows is systemic racism, often overlooked or disregarded, as we tend to assume credit analysis is unbiased. Unfortunately, Adela became another victim of discrimination, excluded from the economic and financial system, rendering her powerless and marginalized.

This story highlights the harsh reality for individuals like Adela, who encounter systemic barriers that impede their progress despite following all the prescribed steps. It is a stark reminder that we must confront and address the pervasive issues of discrimination and exclusion, working for a fairer and more equitable economic landscape for all.

The US financial system has a long history of exhibiting bias against women borrowers. When a woman, especially if she belongs to a different racial or ethnic group than the lender, approaches a bank for a loan, the likelihood of being denied increases. This phenomenon can be attributed to what is commonly referred to as "implicit bias." Banks often perceive women of color as having higher credit risks due to lower income (resulting from the gender wage gap) and the assumption that women may lack proficiency in managing a business. These biased judgments stem from the credit models used by banks and their underlying implicit prejudices against women (Smith 2023).

Unfortunately, if you are a woman entrepreneur, you are likely paying a higher interest rate for your business loan. You were approved for a smaller amount or offered a shorter loan term than your male counterparts. In fact, being a woman makes you more likely to get rejected for a business loan. If your application is accepted, the collateral requirements will be more stringent, too (Arraiz 2022).

At first, I did not know how to help Adela after the banks denied her the microloan. However, after reviewing what we built together, such as the financial projections and a drafted business plan, I knew they were sound, and the business could be created. What mattered was I believed in Adela and her ability. She would make it happen. Her vision was clear and self-assured.

My dilemma was I would take on the financial risk and had yet to start a business. I tried to start a couple of businesses, but they failed in the startup phase because I could not raise the capital. Consequently, I did not want that to happen to Adela. Again, I recalled my parents asking for help to start their business, and I was too young to help, but now I was in a position to help Adela. I had savings I could draw from to give her to start the business. It was a leap of faith. I knew Adela had no choice but to succeed, or her family would be jeopardized and suffer significant financial hardship. I made a promise to serve her and the community. I was not going to back down.

I invited Adela and her husband to my house in Pacifica. I told Adela, "I have decided to give you my savings to start your business. Would you accept my check for $10,000?" Adela was in utter shock and speechless. She hugged me tightly and said, "I gratefully accept the money and promise to pay you back." I explained I had three conditions, "First, you will allow me to teach you some additional business techniques about bookkeeping, business management, and leadership. Second, you will let me become your community partner in the business. Lastly, you will let me document what happened to you regarding the financial institutions, so it does not happen to others." She agreed, and we got started.

Problem Statement

We are all part of a socioeconomic system that enables the unleashing of human potential. Unfortunately for many of us, we are unable to reach our potential due to economic, racial, and gender inequalities that exist in the socioeconomic system. The barriers to women starting and maintaining a successful business include lack of startup capital, business resources, gender discrimination within male-dominated sectors, little access to networks, difficulty obtaining government contracts, and children and family obligations (Buttle 2021). Compound these barriers with the wealth inequality that exists in the US.

The wealth divide is significant if we look at net worth between races and measure a person's assets minus their liabilities. The median net worth of Whites is eight times that of Black families. In 2021, for every dollar a White family had in wealth, a Black family had twenty-three cents, and a Hispanic family had nineteen cents (Hernandez Kent and Perkis 2022). We will dive deeper into net worth later in the book because it is a critical component of the economic development of generational wealth-building created from entrepreneurship. However, regardless of these systemic challenges, women and BIPOC entrepreneurs forge forward with grit and passion for seeing their dreams of owning their small businesses realized.

In the last fifteen years, African Americans and Latinx have emerged as the fastest-growing demographic segment demonstrating the highest rates of entrepreneurship. The leaders among these two groups are women. African American women lead the entrepreneurial growth, and close behind are Latinx women. Between 1996 and 2015, the minority share of businesses increased from 23 to 39 percent; women of color launched seven out of ten new businesses.

A *Harvard Business Review* report states that 17 percent of Black women are in the process of starting or running new businesses, compared to just 10 percent of White women and 15 percent of White men. Only 3 percent of overall entrepreneurs can sustain their businesses, and most self-fund because they cannot access capital as a leading cause to sustaining business maturity. On average, White-led firms generate ten times the revenue of Black-led firms and eight times that of Latinx firms. While people of color make up 39 percent of the US population, they receive access to less than 5 percent of Fortune 100 contracts and less than 2 percent of government contracts (Harvard Business Review 2021).

Also, Latinx businesses grew 34 percent in the last ten years, according to the *2021 State of Latino Entrepreneurship* research report (Gomez-Aguinaga 2022).

For Latinx and African American families, micro- or small-business ownership offers an opportunity to achieve financial stability, build generational wealth, sustain household income, and contribute to their community's positive economic and social benefits. Owning your own business creates a path to independence. This stability flows efficiently from entrepreneurs to their families to their neighborhoods, transforming entire communities. These businesses employ families. If the business successfully sells its products and services to the community, then the community will support the business for years and sometimes generations. A well-run micro- or small business generates profit, grows, and thrives with its community. The owner can reinvest the profit into the business for growth and invest in its staff. Micro- and small business becomes a source of wealth creation, accumulated assets, and job creation (Klein and Wayman 2008).

Entrepreneurship—A Proven Pathway to Financial Stability

The US economic development system needs innovation, social justice, and racial equity. This is precisely what I was compelled to develop with my team. We help lead the socioeconomic change by promoting fair and equitable systems to access capital, entrepreneurship education, and coaching.

We have learned that innovation, entrepreneurial drive, and talent are distributed equally, regardless of race or gender. Unfortunately, due to systemic racism and bias in the economic development system, the opportunity, innovation, and entrepreneurial spirit are lost.

New entrepreneurs with innovative ideas are everywhere, especially in racially-diverse ethnic groups in underserved communities. As a society, we need to examine the efforts being made by the government and the private sector to uncover and address systemic racial gaps and biases in the entrepreneurial ecosystems in a way that provides inclusivity and support for the diversity of entrepreneurs that bring economic and social value to our communities and elevate our way of life.

Entrepreneurship and microenterprise development are proven wealth-building strategies for low-income and minority communities trying to lift themselves out of poverty (Klein and Wayman 2008). Especially for historically disadvantaged women, business creation is among the best ways to become independent and financially secure. Entrepreneurship can close the racial wealth gap and create economic mobility.

It is more important than ever to reduce barriers, provide equal economic opportunity and make it easier for entrepreneurs of color to start and grow businesses. Creating inclusive and equitable entrepreneurship ecosystems is essential to revitalize the economic development system to promote equal access. We need to work together to present entrepreneurship as a clear pathway to business creation and support services so that business ownership can be a reality and create jobs in our communities.

Madam C.J. Walker, the first self-made female African American millionaire, embodies the entrepreneurial spirit I talk about. She was born in 1867 on the same Louisiana plantation where her parents, Owen and Minerva Anderson Breedlove, were enslaved before the end of the Civil War. She was a child of sharecroppers that transformed herself from an uneducated farm laborer and launderer into one of the twentieth century's most successful women entrepreneurs (George 2019).

According to the *Guinness Book of World Records*, she says, "I am a woman who came from the cotton fields of the South. From there, I was promoted to the washtub. From there, I was promoted to the cook kitchen. And from there, I promoted myself into the business of manufacturing hair goods and preparations. I have built my own factory on my own ground" (Stephenson 2021).

Inspired by Adela and the legacy of Madam C.J. Walker, Centro Community Partners (Centro) was founded in 2010 as an Oakland-based 501(c)(3) nonprofit. Centro supports low-income entrepreneurs and entrepreneurship ecosystems in the US, Latin America, and Africa. We provide entrepreneurship education, access to capital, and coaching to entrepreneurs. We also offer educational systems and know-how to other nonprofits to build their capacity and grow their community impact. Our services teach individuals to exercise their self-determination and break the cycle of poverty through their entrepreneurial spirit, resulting in a thriving community.

Summary

Today, our economic development system may be plagued by injustice, bias, and discrimination; however, we hold the power to shape a better future by creating new systems that promote equal access and economic opportunity. Entrepreneurship is a pathway to financial stability and empowerment. Women entrepreneurs, in particular, drive the charge in the entrepreneurial landscape, and we must support and empower them. They can usher in the next era of economic prosperity in the US.

Adela's vision for her childcare service ignited a passion within me and inspired the founding of Centro. Motivated by a deep commitment to social justice and driven by personal experiences of discrimination Adela and my parents faced, I embarked on a journey to become a leader in creating social justice in economic development. Centro, our microenterprise development organization, was born out of my commitment to serve women entrepreneurs of color whom the existing economic development system has marginalized. Guided by core principles of racial justice, gender equity, and social justice, we work tirelessly to build community-based services that cater to this underserved population.

We must act now if we genuinely aspire to witness significant positive change within our generation. We must develop a comprehensive plan to bring about the transformative shifts needed to foster a more inclusive and equitable society.

Key Lessons

- *Make lemonade from lemons. Embracing resilience and turning adversity into opportunity is essential in combating systemic racism within the institutional systems that shape our daily lives. It requires courage to stand for your beliefs and move forward with determination.*
- *Volunteering or assisting those in need benefits others and leads to personal growth and empowerment. By giving of yourself, you gain a deeper understanding of your capabilities and contribute to the success and well-being of others.*
- *Real change in systems, communities, or the world often arises from personal experiences that profoundly impact us negatively. These firsthand encounters give us the understanding and motivation to develop unique solutions to economic and social challenges.*
- *Women entrepreneurs play a crucial role in shaping the future of the US economy and closing the gender gap. To achieve this, they require access to capital, mentors, and comprehensive entrepreneurship education. If existing systems fail to provide these resources, we must build new, inclusive systems that empower and support women in their entrepreneurial endeavors.*

CHAPTER 2

SMALL BUSINESS DEVELOPMENT SYSTEM: CHALLENGES AND SOLUTIONS

The government's Small Business Administration reports that small businesses represent 99 percent of all employers in the US and are responsible for generating well over half of the new jobs created.

—ELLEN O'KANE TAUSCHER

If small businesses are crucial to the US economy, why don't we require entrepreneurship, financial literacy, and business planning classes in high school? Kids start businesses too, right? Did you run a business in high school? I started my first business in middle school. My friend Greg and I would make caramel corn and sell hand-sized balls for one dollar each. It supplemented the allowance my parents gave me.

Nothing easier than selling candy as a kid to other kids. It was my first side gig before I could legally work. Gig work has evolved and is taking us in new directions.

It is 10 a.m. in San Francisco on a weekday in September, and Fernanda delivers food to the homes of paying clients. She is a gig worker for DoorDash, a food delivery service. She shares her story with me as we visit grocery stores and restaurants. She says, "Inflation makes life harder on me. Gas prices are crazy high and so expensive that I need to work longer hours."

Fernanda, an immigrant from Colombia, attends San Francisco State University full-time. She handles her food deliveries carefully and is kind and cheerful with her customers as she hands them their orders. She shares how grateful she is to be a gig worker because it helped to support her and her family in Colombia and pay her tuition.

Over the last year, I have met many gig workers, like Uber drivers, that use gig work to make ends meet or become more financially stable. Most gig workers I meet already have full-time jobs, but those jobs don't pay enough to make ends meet, so gig work is their solution. I am impressed with the gig worker platforms because they are egalitarian-based and have transformed how people work through self-employment.

How can we transform our small business development system to be egalitarian? It would treat people equally and give them more opportunities.

A Look at Business Ownership by Race in US Population

Small business ownership is a proven source to increase household income leading to financial independence. PayScale reports that the median income of $66,373 is generated from self-employed owners representing incorporated small businesses (PayScale 2023).

As a catalyst to wealth-building, small businesses also benefit the community by promoting economic growth, job creation, and a higher quality of life. Small businesses are defined by the SBA as having less than 500 employees, which is most of the businesses in the US. However, when we examine the statistics of business ownership, we can see the racial divide among small business owners as it relates to the percentage of the US population. The following table shows that Whites have 78.3 percent of US businesses, representing 60.1 percent of the US population. Compared to Black-owned businesses at 11.7 percent of all businesses representing 13.4 percent, and Hispanic businesses at 14.4 percent, representing 18.5 percent of the population.

What solution could be offered to close this gap?

Table 1

Race/Ethnicity of Business Owner	# of Businesses	% of all Businesses	% with Employees	% of US Population
Asian	557,835	7.70%	10.10%	5.90%
Black	3,075,551	11.70%	2.20%	13.40%
Hispanic	3,966,625	14.40%	5.80%	18.50%
Native American	108,933	0.30%	0.40%	1.30%
White	26,978,211	78.29%	81.02%	60.10%

Source: US Census Annual Business Survey 2018

This problem is further exacerbated among women who continue to face barriers when starting or growing small businesses and accessing capital and networks essential for their growth and support.

The Urban Institute shows that only 4.4 percent of all dollars lent have gone to women-owned businesses. Women entrepreneurs get 2.5 times less total capital than men; on average, women get $59,857 while men receive $156,279, but also, women borrowers have to pay higher interest rates for smaller-sized business loans (The Urban Institute 2008).

Given the racial disparities among business owners, how can we make business ownership more accessible to underserved entrepreneurs of color? What is the root cause of the racial disparity? If our US economy is based on small businesses, we should prioritize access to capital, entrepreneurship education, and financial literacy training for all people. Business ownership increases income, economic empowerment, and wealth creation. Access to the building blocks such as tools, resources, and education required to start and grow a small business would enable our communities to thrive.

Small Business Infrastructure Challenges

Unfortunately, discrimination and systemic racism exist within financial institutions. Still, there are more issues to uncover about accessing capital and the infrastructure of the small business development ecosystem. According to Ebetuel "Beto" Pallares, PhD, venture capitalist chair of entrepreneurship at New Mexico State University and president & CEO of Joseph Advisory Services, "We live in a time that there exists more capital for small business creation than ever before. An aspect of the problem is how the capital is organized. The data used to make key policy decisions in Washington is four or five years old. Current information does not exist. We need current data to determine the small business type, size, and the sectors in which they exist." The lack of timely small business information affects the form of capital that can be deployed and how it is best distributed to small- and microenterprises startups.

The ecosystem is critical to meet the demand for small business creation and entrepreneur development. By contrast, if you look at the venture capital model, you see they not only give capital in exchange for equity (i.e., percentage of business ownership) but also provide professional development through leadership and management coaching to the entrepreneurs or startup teams. In the US, there is a strong cultural tendency to think about the individual entrepreneur rather than a collaborative ecosystem used to fund small businesses. However, when we look at the current small business development model, this does not exist in one place. Entrepreneurs of small businesses may not know where to get coaching, and most are unaware of the Community Development Financial Institutions (CDFI), a US government-sponsored and regulated small business lending system, or Kiva, a crowd-sourcing platform for microloans. Instead, they must go to different sources to get the necessary resources, such as entrepreneurship education or mentorship, causing an ecosystem infrastructure problem.

Friends and family could help with part of the capital needs of starting a small business, but it is difficult if you are from a low-income community and your friends and family barely make ends meet. Beto further says that one of the most significant investment gaps in the current US economic development system is between $5,000 and $25,000. Low-income aspiring entrepreneurs of color have unique challenges, such as low saving rates, limited credit, and few or no assets to use as loan collateral. Having no alternatives, these underrepresented entrepreneurs rely on high-interest credit cards to access the startup and working capital they need for their businesses, only to fail and be left with mounting debt. This capital gap causes a loss of productivity, jobs, upside investment potential, and income taxes. The lack of access to capital in the $5,000 to $25,000 range and business coaching services presents a significant unmet need and a unique opportunity to provide microfinance (startup loans) and venture capital (equity).

Therefore, there are four major infrastructure challenges to be solved.

1. Access to capital between $5,000 and $25,000
2. Access to entrepreneurship education, financial literacy, and coaching
3. Access to markets
4. The absence of timely small business data to better understand the demand for services to micro- and small businesses to inform US policymakers.

A possible solution could be a technology-based egalitarian system able to address these challenges.

Centro Community Partners—A Socioeconomic Community Solution

Innovation, entrepreneurial desire, and motivation are distributed equally regardless of race, ethnicity, or socio-economics, but the opportunity and business resources to exercise that entrepreneurial spirit are not.

What about a socioeconomic community solution that empowers low-to-moderate-income entrepreneurs of color with equitable access to a virtual hub of entrepreneurship resources and capital in the community?

I am talking about Centro Community Partners (Centro). We fuel the imagination and prepare low-income entrepreneurs by providing them with entrepreneurship education, access to capital resources, mentorship, and financial literacy. Centro bridges the racial gap in microenterprise development and solves two of the four infrastructure challenges. Founded in Oakland, California, in 2010, Centro's socioeconomic change mission is to serve the underserved low-income communities of women, immigrants, and Black, Indigenous, and people of color (BIPOC) to build small businesses leading to economic empowerment and financial well-being. By upholding the principles of racial equity and social justice in economic opportunity and financial inclusion for all people, Centro has helped more than 8,300 and provided $6.3 million in access to capital (Centro Community Partners 2023).

We cannot afford to let the racial gaps in the economic development system keep talented and passionate entrepreneurs, driven by the entrepreneurship spirit, from realizing dreams that would otherwise benefit their communities.

We developed a steps-to-prosperity model that begins with the idea that all individuals can break the cycle of poverty and build thriving communities through entrepreneurship. They can thrive if they have access to educational tools and financial literacy knowledge tailored to their needs and are culturally appropriate. Centro's program results prove that developing healthy micro- and small businesses, particularly those owned and run by low-income and underserved individuals, is one of the most effective sources of economic and social benefits. These benefits flow efficiently from entrepreneurs to families and neighbors, transforming entire communities. This theory of change forms the basis of all the programs we develop.

Centro also incorporates an open-sourced, asset-based capacity-building approach for community organizations interested in paving new ground in entrepreneurial spaces. This national deployment strategy is designed to increase capacity and expertise amongst community development organizations.

By learning from our mistakes, we created a unique entrepreneurship training model and utilized mobile technology, human center design techniques, and a learning management system. The Centro Business Planning App is central to its deployment strategy, which focuses on increasing entrepreneurial capacity and content understanding across nonprofits working in underserved communities. There are many barriers for low-income entrepreneurs to meet the minimum threshold requirements even to be considered for a microloan by a CDFI. Many CDFIs may not have enough resources to effectively work with communities of color. On the other hand, many community organizations diligently work in communities of color on a broad spectrum of social justice issues, have trusted relationships, and are helpful guidance providers. Unfortunately, many community-based organizations may lack the expertise to support entrepreneurship programs within their services. Centro's national deployment strategy changes that by providing other community-based organizations access to Centro's free app, virtual entrepreneurship curriculum, and training to bridge the gaps in the economic development systems.

Entrepreneurs who complete a Centro program can access business resources to start and grow their small businesses and positively impact their community by creating jobs and financial well-being for themselves and their families. One example is Ayanna, who went through the Centro program, and five months later, she could access capital and started her Pilates studio HEAL in Albany, California. She offers services that are therapeutic, accessible, and tailored to the needs of the individual client. Ayanna is a passionate, form-based instructor who treats her classes like workshops and helps her clients to heal. She was also able to employ others to work at her studio.

What if entrepreneurship education could be scaled to anyone who wants to start and grow a new business? The SBA says about 70 percent of new businesses survive past the first two years, 50 percent operate after five years, and 30 percent after ten years. Therefore, what can help new entrepreneurs improve their chances of business survival (Commerce Institute 2023)?

A nonprofit-sponsored entrepreneurship education and financial literacy program can significantly improve a new entrepreneur's chances of survival and business success over the long term (Klein and Wayman 2008). First, community-based programs, like Centro's, teach new entrepreneurs to think critically about their business idea and help them to develop a working and adaptive business model. Second, the program is designed to ask the tough questions: Why do you want to start a business? Why are you the best person to provide the service or product? How do you differentiate yourself from the competition? How much are your startup costs? What is your break-even point? Trained facilitators create a safe and lively interactive environment where the entrepreneurship training program can occur online or in person. In this nurturing and safe environment, entrepreneurs can learn from each other, open themselves up to new ideas, and develop a growth mindset. As a result, we see their capacities grow, enabling them to be better prepared to start a business.

Centro offers culturally and linguistically relevant services for low-income people who speak Spanish and English through an app and programs. In contrast, the SBA provides services to people with access to computers, and digital skills, who speak English and have higher educational attainment.

This new knowledge and awareness allow new entrepreneurs to better understand the costs of starting their businesses and learn to save money to reach their financial goals.

Entrepreneurs also look at their spending habits, manage debt, and work on improving their credit scores. New entrepreneurs that complete an entrepreneurship education program benefit from creating a robust business plan with financial projections and are better equipped to manage risk. They are also introduced to an ecosystem of nonprofit business support services critical to the entrepreneurs' journey as they start their new businesses.

Remember Adela? She repaid the $10,000. She opened Adela's World of the Children in 2009, a licensed childcare center offering daycare and pre-kindergarten for El Cerrito, Berkeley, and Oakland families. By providing a balance of play and learning based on her early childhood curriculum, Adela demonstrates how much she cares for the children in her center. After many years, her business continues to thrive in her community. Not only does it prepare the World of the Children students for their future, but it also helps Adela send her children to college. More than anything, her business has brought joy and meaning to her life and those around her.

In 2022, Adela partnered with Centro again, using the Centro Capital Hub to access Kiva's crowd-funding platform. She successfully acquired an interest-free loan to upgrade and expand her business assets. Adela said, "This loan allows me to purchase new and updated materials and equipment, renovate the location, and make it more attractive to new clients." These funds will help Adela remodel the daycare with new toys and outdoor activities. They will also be used to hire an additional caregiver to ensure the children continue to receive the attention and care Adela's World is known for. "This loan will have a great and positive impact on my business because not only will I be able to create a fun and engaging place for our children, but I will also be able to maintain the business I have worked so hard on for many years. We have served over eighty children since we opened our doors in 2009."

We can learn a lot from Adela's experience and entrepreneurial spirit. Inspiration drives change. My team and I are passionate about building more organizations like Adela's, which are part of thriving communities.

Summary

Despite the systemic racism that has led to racial disparities in business ownership and the existing gaps within the economic system, some resilient low-income entrepreneurs are determined to start their businesses. Nonprofit microenterprise development organizations like Centro are crucial in addressing these challenges. They have tailored their programs to meet the specific needs of this target population, resulting in a significant positive impact on both the entrepreneurs and the communities they serve.

While Centro acknowledges that it is still a work in progress and continues to learn and grow, its unwavering focus on its mission drives the organization to strive for continuous improvement. Centro is committed to inspiring curiosity and supporting new change makers in launching their social enterprises, which contribute to the betterment of humanity and the advancement of peace and equity.

We invite you to join us in this journey and collaborate to create a world of positive change. Mahatma Gandhi wisely said, "In a gentle way, you can shake the world."

Key Lessons

- *Empowering entrepreneurs with financial literacy skills is crucial for their success, enabling them to navigate the world of capital access. This involves understanding financial statements, budgeting, bookkeeping, and credit scores.*
- *Transforming the small and micro business development system from a fragmented model to a centralized hub and bespoke virtual system design can streamline the provision of capital, entrepreneurship education, and coaching services, making it more accessible and efficient.*
- *Although the absence of up-to-date data hinders capital providers from organizing and developing improved financial products tailored to small and micro businesses' needs, Centro has started collecting data to help fill this gap.*
- *More data is needed to improve the implementation of effective government policies aimed at enhancing the infrastructure and support systems for small business development.*
- *Prioritizing demand-side development involves identifying and facilitating better sources of capital to foster the growth and expansion of small businesses.*

CHAPTER 3

GUIDING PRINCIPLES AND THE PATH FORWARD

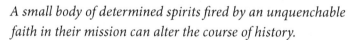

A small body of determined spirits fired by an unquenchable faith in their mission can alter the course of history.

—MAHATMA GANDHI

Guiding Principles

Do you know where you are headed in your walk of life? How do you create the path forward when you start a nonprofit or a social enterprise? What directs your actions, prioritizes your resources, and assists your decision-making?

To help me with these tough questions, I created guiding principles that would become a part of the organization's mission, vision, and shared values.

When I founded Centro, I knew I needed guiding principles. Generally, well-thought-out principles galvanize the organization and aid in the staff's focus on both the vision and mission; they also serve as a guiding force to direct the organization and team through good and bad times. I remember writing several different guiding principles, but all sounded rather corny and fell short of the feeling and guidance I needed for Centro. As an exercise, I would practice saying them to trusted friends to gauge their reactions. I aimed to explicitly state that the guiding principles were values-based, mission-focused, and community-oriented.

Centro was founded on the principle of racial and gender equity and social justice, allowing low-income individuals to be enabled and empowered to contribute significantly to their community's economic, social, and spiritual well-being. It took several iterations to nail them down, but when I finally settled on Centro's guiding principles, I confirmed this was the path Centro would take.

"The vision: To enable entrepreneurs to build their dreams, offer a new community-based approach to investing, and bring purposeful volunteers together for the greater good."

"The mission: To invest in people, build microenterprises, and strengthen local communities to improve people's lives."

"The shared values: Respect for All, Community Service, and Excellence in our Work."

These three principles helped to answer the tough questions of whom we are helping, why we are helping them, and how we will help them. They provided a solid foundation to start upon and helped me to organize and align Centro's entrepreneurship educational programs, recruit staff/volunteers, and help beneficiaries.

If the organization is to serve the community, then these principles must demonstrate the heart and soul of the organization. They act like a beacon attracting the new talent needed to develop an impactful and effective team and bring the beneficiaries and other stakeholders from the community for partnership, such as funders and other nonprofits.

Constructing the Vision, Mission & Shared Values

Keep the mission and vision simple, short, and memorable. This means no more than one sentence. Organizations with a wordy mission statement are problematic because the staff might not remember it. The mission and vision statements answer the questions about identity (who we are), purpose (what we value), and direction (where we are headed). A report by Bain and Company shows that about 90 percent of top firms have mission and vision statements (Bart and Baetz 1998). They also found that they were well communicated, understood, and collectively shared, resulting in better performance than organizations without them (Bart, Bontis, and Taggar 2001, 19–35).

To guide your path forward, use guiding principles that include the mission, vision, and shared values as the three critical components when starting your organization. These three components are necessary for the organization to maintain direction and motivation and to avoid diverging from its intended target and failing to create impact. It is reasonable that in the course of organizational development, these three components change and evolve. They are expected to change over time, but they should always be in place to guide your organization.

As you develop your organization, the leader should ask themselves the following questions:

- What are my values?
- What will be my mission and our organization's mission?
- Does the vision focus on you or your organization?

In the case of Centro, our mission, vision, and values have evolved as the organization has matured. However, our shared values since our inception, such as service to the community and empowering others to reach their dreams of business ownership, remain the same. For example, Centro's mission has changed to:

"To build thriving communities by providing underserved, low-income women and Black, Indigenous, and people of color (BIPOC) with entrepreneurship education, financial literacy, coaching and access to capital."

The mission defines our reason for being and clearly explains what our organization will do daily to achieve its vision. Our vision has also changed over the years and reads as follows:

"Create a racially just and equitable economic development system for entrepreneurship to thrive."

What is the difference between a mission and a vision statement? The distinction is essential. The mission statement describes what you do, whom you do it for, and the benefit it provides. It is usually a short statement that all employees can easily recite and remember. The vision should be worded so that it provides guidance and inspiration. It is a forward-thinking statement that should be fulfilled in the future.

As the founder, I have my values of family, integrity, empathy, community, social justice, love of learning, and racial harmony. However, Centro's staff has shared organizational values which evolved over the years and included the following:

"We value innovation, diversity, inclusion, freedom, collaboration, and equity."

These shared organizational values communicate publicly what the team values. They also guide how the staff interacts, creates, and leads. As the organization comes together, it becomes a collection of the contributions of the staff and volunteers in it. As the change maker, it is advisable to learn how to incorporate the best values from the team and make them a part of the overall shared values.

Leadership Development

If you start a nonprofit or social enterprise, you are probably passionate and want to serve your community, as I did. You are on your way to becoming a leader. Perhaps you are called to community work or social impact work because you have witnessed or personally experienced the injustices in our society or its degrading environmental realities. Social change leaders come from all walks of life but share a common thread: they do not accept the world as it is. Instead, they work tirelessly to build a better world for everyone. This is why it is vital to express the feelings and drive in the mission and vision statements so it can channel the passion and spirit to guide your team and serve the community well.

My experience as a nonprofit leader and change maker has taught me to focus my passion and intention on the mission and vision of the organization. It is natural to feel compassionate and empathize with the community that needs serving. As a child of immigrants from Peru, I had a natural affinity with immigrants, especially those from countries torn up by war or economic instability. They always reminded me of my parents, who struggled once they got to the US but, over the years, were able to stabilize economically and flourish.

A leader learns how to access the resources and develop staff to positively impact the target community. They lead by example as a force of positive change and architect new systems that benefit and include the underserved. To realize such change, an organization, either a nonprofit or a for-profit social enterprise, must be created. The leader will make significant personal and professional sacrifices and often be compensated less given their education, skill, ability, and intellect. They will seldom be recognized or acknowledged for their change-making efforts and societal contributions. If you embark on this journey, you must face the realities of the sacrifices that will be necessary to make. Like any other profession, social leaders endure the trials and tribulations of creating change with time. Their ideas can positively change communities, countries, and the world.

During my first two years starting Centro, I had yet to learn what I got myself into. In February 2010, I started building Centro with a grant from my first funder, and I had eighteen months to show success. I was excited and scared. I had no experience running a nonprofit and did not know when I would get another grant. Regardless, I was chosen to lead this unique nonprofit organization. It was my calling, and I wanted to rise to the challenge. Failure was not an option, although it did occur frequently.

When you engage in a startup, a personal transformation happens. Although I did not have any nonprofit experience, I did have other leadership experience in different industries. I led teams before in my role at global consulting companies, the wine industry, and financial institutions. However, I was really out of my element in a community-based organization. Therefore, I learned fast. I gave up my free time. I worked weekends and holidays and didn't take time off for three years. I was on a steep learning curve. Being passionate about the community work of serving others is very supportive and well-aligned with my life's purpose. It was an incredible experience, and I would do it again. I was living my purpose, and everything flowed harmoniously. Even today, it still feels like that despite the many mistakes I still make—these are lessons well-learned.

The Emotional Side of the Startup Phase

The startup phase was my crucible. During this phase, I could feel transformation take place in me, too. During the first three years of the startup phase, the loneliness was the toughest to manage and get through. After teaching my

Friday classes with the volunteer business advisors, I would go home to Pacifica from Oakland via the metro train. I would sometimes break down and cry after exiting the station to walk to my car. Walking across the sky bridge, I hoped nobody would see me or notice my tears. There was no one to reassure me that I was doing the right thing or that the sacrifices of time were worth it. My family was supportive, but not sure why I chose to go into nonprofit community work and away from my career in management consulting. My family did not want to see me struggle financially because of the hefty student loan burden from graduate school that I carried. I always questioned myself but relied on my faith when I turned to God. I prayed for wisdom, strength, and perseverance to continue moving Centro forward as I kept its mission in my heart, and slowly my spiritual power grew.

Fortunately, the intensity of my weekly emotional breakdown sessions waned, and I had a breakthrough. I reached the other side of a new phase in my life. I developed a greater capacity for the leadership role. My capacity for patience, compassion, and empathy also grew. I began to feel more secure in myself and Centro's future. My insecurities at the beginning of the startup phase disappeared and were replaced with positive, affirming thoughts about growing the organization.

I understood why the mission, vision, and shared values were so important and now became greater than me. My transformation process broke me down. This process humbled me to serve the community and the entrepreneurial beneficiaries better. I opened myself up to be transparent and a guide to our clients. My "being" helped me to hold space and be a mirror. In the Centro program, I wanted my entrepreneur students to see themselves as they were—powerful and self-aware with endless creativity, capable of becoming successful entrepreneurs. They just started their journey of becoming business owners and financially securing their families' welfare which thriving communities are built upon.

Change happens as part of the transformation. Looking at the context of social change for the greater good, we can see many examples that prove anything is possible. Ethical leaders ask fundamental questions about the human experience. They ask why societies allow for oppression, injustices, and inequities. By starting a nonprofit or social enterprise, you are explicitly working to solve the problems most important to you, your target population, and your community. Pursuing your cause will create transformative moments for yourself, your team, and the beneficiaries.

Summary

I hope you understand why guiding principles will help you navigate before you start your social impact organization. They are foundational to the organization, and research shows their importance to its development. These guiding principles come in various forms. We discussed creating a clear and concise mission, a forward-looking vision, and a collection of shared organizational values to get started. You will be well-equipped once you explicitly draft these guiding principles.

Next is to take stock of yourself. Transformation happens to those who lead an organization for social change. It starts when you least expect it, and your ability to adapt to your identity or a self-discovery of your true nature could emerge and grow. Each day in your social enterprise or nonprofit will challenge or reward you. Your capacity will undoubtedly grow, and you will begin to thrive in your new organization.

Key Lessons

- *Your mission needs to be kept simple and memorable.*
- *The vision is the future state of the world you would like to see realized. It is like the bull's eye that you aim for in your day-to-day operations.*
- *Personal and shared values are the glue that keeps you and your staff engaged in the mission and vision.*
- *Accept that transformation is part of the journey of the social change maker. It is necessary to burn off insecurities, self-doubt, and old habits that do not enable you to reach higher levels of self-awareness or skill.*
- *Understand what you will give up or sacrifice to see the desired change. Social change leadership is not for the faint of heart; you must sacrifice on many levels to succeed.*

CHAPTER 4

START WITH A PLAN

———— ✦◇✦ ————

It's not how much we give, but how much love we put into giving.

—MOTHER TERESA

Have you attempted to embark on a meaningful endeavor without a plan? If so, you probably discovered that achieving significant results is nearly impossible when you lack the necessary resources, such as capital, people, and a clear understanding of the needs. My older brother, Rolando, who established his architectural design small business at a young age, always emphasized the importance of having a plan. He firmly believed significance could only be accomplished with a well-thought-out roadmap, especially in writing. And his successful experiences have shown me the truth behind his words.

What if we could replicate the model that worked for Adela? I asked myself if it could serve her, then I could help others like her in the community. I had an invisible force divinely guiding me. I was strongly driven to do something. It was urgent. I kept telling myself this organization needed to exist because many entrepreneurs were left out and discriminated against daily. In my heart, I knew it was the right thing to do, and I needed to stay the course no matter what lay ahead.

After helping Adela launch her business in September 2009, I was inspired to take the idea of providing business training to the next level. Using Adela's business as a sample case study, I started to draft a business plan called Centro Community Partners. I was so excited. I could not sleep much for a month until it was done. I chose the name to be Centro Community Partners to represent the "business center" in Spanish, combined with the idea of "trusted connection" through a partnership with the community.

I was grateful something extraordinary took place during the moments that Centro was coming to be. My heart is filled with love and devotion to Centro. The divine inspiration humbled me. As I wrote, I often thought of my parents and how much I missed them, especially since my mother's death, and my relationship with my dad had become distant since then. But I am close to them in spirit. In my heart, I knew this new journey I was embarking on with Centro would not be one I would take alone. Instead, I would be accompanied by God and the spirit of my Peruvian indigenous ancestors guiding me in each step. My faith grew during this experience.

A significant change started in me. I felt a fire ignite in me, showing me the way. I was lost at the beginning of 2009 but found my way out of my despair. I felt profound satisfaction and happiness as I created Centro's plan. I was on the path to becoming the person I imagined I could be—to serve others. Thanks to Centro, I became empowered.

By the end of 2009, the Centro plan was done. But who would read the plan? Who would help me, and who would fund my social impact idea?

I was confident about the facts. There was a strong demand for advanced entrepreneurship training and coaching services due to a void in the local economic development ecosystem. I wanted to solve the four areas where the infrastructure for small business creation was broken. There were four gap areas, including access to capital between $5,000 and $25,000, business education/coaching, access to markets, and timely small business data to understand the demand of micro- and small businesses to advise policymakers. But instead, I first focused on creating a solid, replicable business/entrepreneurship education and coaching model. My original plan was to incorporate microequity as the access to the capital component. I needed to put that idea on the back burner to keep my focus.

Raising Money

I was fearful of raising the money to start up a nonprofit. My fear came from having previously sought funding for two other ventures and being told no. Centro would be a social benefit corporation to serve low-income people of color in the community, but I needed experience with such an enterprise. I failed to launch two for-profit businesses ten years prior that were opposites—a winery and an investment company—but at least I had experience in both industries. Those were promising investment ventures, but finding capital as a person of color was difficult. This caused great internal negativity. Regardless, I had to change my mindset and attitude if I was going to pitch Centro.

The right mindset to raise money for a social impact idea is key to successful execution. To fund the Centro mission, I needed to become a fundraiser. I had to get comfortable asking people for money. I was passionate about the work done with Adela, and I was excited about helping more people realize their entrepreneurship dreams. Furthermore, I thought asking for money was the last thing I wanted or was comfortable doing, but I overcame my fear because the money was not for me; it was for the community. Recognizing the need to switch from ego to serving others enabled me to face my fear. In the past, my fear was rooted in a reflection of my ego and my business idea. Centro, however, was not about me but rather about the community and righting the wrongs in our economic development system so that low-income people of color could be served. The love to serve others became the liberating factor, and the fear gave way.

Centro's First Believer & Funder

In December 2009, I called the Oakland Business Development Corporation (OBDC) (now named Mainstreet Launch) to request a meeting with Jacob Singer, its chief executive officer. OBDC is one of the oldest community development financial institutions in Oakland. I discovered Jacob was an alumnus of the Peter F. Drucker School of Management in Claremont and a student of Peter F. Drucker, known as the father of modern management. We shared this in common. I admired Jacob's career and respected his experience in equity and small business finance. I remember being so excited to meet him and share my experiences with Peter, but I also sought his guidance and wisdom. He was a leader of a non-profit financial institution that was helping to provide small business loans to underserved entrepreneurs in the community. I was eager to present him with the Centro business plan and to get his feedback. I was not expecting much more than his unique perspective.

During our first meeting, Jacob was tall, intellectual, and had a softness to his manner. He kindly extended his hand to shake mine and greet me. "So how can I help you?" he asked me.

"Well, I came to explain something that recently happened to me regarding an immigrant woman entrepreneur named Adela who wanted to start a child daycare service. She applied for a microloan at OBDC, but unfortunately, she was denied."

Jacob's interest was piqued, and he asked, "Oh? Do you know why?"

I said, "Yeah, she was told that because she had no credit history, OBDC could not lend to her. Since the CDFIs didn't want to lend to her, I decided to lend Adela the $10,000 she needed to start her business, and we were able to launch her daycare service in a month." I also shared that Adela filled out her client list and started making income.

He was surprised to hear I lent her the money and exclaimed, "Wow! Why would you do that?"

I explained, "I conducted the risk assessment; she was a reasonable investment." I didn't share that Adela reminded me of what happened to my parents when they wanted to start their small business since I met Jacob for the first time.

He politely asked, "How can we help you now?"

"I would love it if you would read this business plan I just completed. I desire to create an advanced training program to help others like Adela who are seeking assistance starting their business."

I smiled and chuckled to myself. Jacob asked, "What's so funny?"

I answered, "Sorry for the long plan. It is about fifty pages. Probably way too long for a business plan, but I wanted to be thorough. In my defense, I wrote more than just a business plan. I also presented the research to support my claims about the problems with our community's current economic development system."

I explained to Jacob how I wanted to innovate the approach to technical assistance and entrepreneurship education and training that could bridge the gaps and introduce new experimental concepts such as microequity community funding of small businesses. Jacob became more curious and showed his interest in reading the business plan.

Jacob said, "I would happily review your plan and provide feedback." I walked up to him, took one deep breath, and handed him the Centro plan. My future hopes and dreams were placed gently in Jacob's hands. He was the right person, and the plan was in the right place. A deep feeling of gratefulness fell over me like a warm blanket. It felt like I was led to Jacob to reach the next critical step. I left his office happy and inspired.

The following day, as I opened my email inbox, I saw a message from Jacob. Surprised to see a response so soon, I nervously opened it. It read, "Hi Arturo, thanks for coming in yesterday. Good to meet you. I just reviewed your business plan. Lots of good stuff, but I still have some questions and concerns...I am starting to form some thoughts about how we might work together, and I am wondering if it might be feasible for OBDC to incubate Centro in some way. Let's schedule lunch to talk about the details." I jumped out of bed excitedly and knelt, praying to God and giving thanks. I was blessed. I reread his email so it would sink in before I could write him back to schedule our next meeting.

He requested I present the Centro pilot program idea to his team at OBDC. Hearing his words got me brainstorming, and my ideas flowed as I prepared the presentation. I arrived early at the OBDC office, and his staff of about six people entered the conference room. I was nervous but took a deep breath and began talking about Adela's daycare business case, how OBDC denied her funding, and how we could work together to help low-income people with similar credit risk issues receive funding. Once I was done, Jacob and the team thanked me. Several team members came to me and said, "Impressive! I hope we can work together. Your ideas inspired me." I said, "Thank you so much. It was an honor to present to you. I was so grateful to show your team how to help underserved women entrepreneurs like Adela."

I left the OBDC office and walked around the downtown Oakland neighborhood before taking the train back home to Pacifica. There would be a one-hour commute from home each day, but it would be worth it. I thought, *Oh my God! I would be starting my life's purpose.* My heart was filled with love, and I mentally thanked Adela for letting me help her. The presentation to the OBDC team lifted my spirits. It was almost like an out-of-body experience. I replayed the presentation in my mind over and over.

The next day, I received a gift. Jacob wrote me and told me the team enjoyed the presentation and offered me a grant of $100,000 for the first year, which would allow for the incubation of Centro Community Partners at OBDC. Incubation in this context means helping a startup business in its infancy succeed by providing workspace, seed funding, mentoring, and training. Jacob would take me under his wing and personally coach and guide me. He offered me an office with a shared conference room where I could provide the entrepreneurship training program to the community. They would also provide access to microloans to the entrepreneurs completing the Centro program. I did it! Centro secured an office, funding, and its first employee—me. Jacob became our first believer and our first funder. I hadn't successfully raised money before that moment.

In the days that followed, I couldn't stop thinking about how the chain of events unfolded beautifully between me, Adela, and Jacob. My initial investment in Adela in August led to an investment in Centro by Jacob in December 2009. Remember that this period was a time of economic despair, and many people lost their jobs after the financial meltdown in 2008. We were in the middle of one of the most significant recessions in US history.

THE PLANNING OF THE PLAN

A basic plan consists of three major components, which help to understand what is needed to do first. The following are the steps in planning.

STEP 1 - USE FACTS TO IDENTIFY THE SOCIAL PROBLEM

Before building a plan, you must understand the scope of the social problem and how one can solve or provide a partial solution which requires conducting research. Many free online research resources offer a social impact leader guidance and insight. You want to create a business case supported by the research of credible individuals who observe the same social problem as you do. This allows you to demonstrate that it's a known and documented problem in which you can use the facts to make your case. Using the facts of the social issues in your business plan, you become credible, knowledgeable, and truthful about what you are talking about. Investors and funders must trust their investments and grants will be used to solve the identified social problem.

STEP 2 - THE PILOT

Next, you can design your solution into a pilot, like how Adela's daycare was Centro's pilot. This test will have minimal costs you need to cover but will provide some results and insight into your ability to solve the problem. A plan that documents your research and your pilot's results will help you see what you know and what you do not know. The gaps start to emerge, and then you can better identify the gaps that must be filled. Again, this is not an exact science, but it is an important exercise to see if your intervention will work. The pilot gives other insights into the costs and funds needed for a large, more expansive program. Knowing how much money you need to get started and how much to sustain operations will be critical for long-term success. This exercise will become the basis of your first year's budget. You can try to project the second year, but it is tough to get close to accuracy due to the number of changing variables in your assumptions about the pilot's results and initial costs.

STEP 3 - WHY ARE YOU BEST TO SOLVE THE SOCIAL PROBLEM?

Credibility is important, but it is trust that wins the money. To get the funds, grantmakers, investors, and philanthropists need to know if they can trust you. They will try to understand whether or not you are honest, passionate, capable of managing money, serving your beneficiaries, and effective in addressing the social problem. Remember that education is considered in the evaluation process but not a requirement for social impact. You need to have lived the experience with the problem you attempt to solve or have work experience as a problem solver or team leader.

The funder will ask you directly why you can do this work. Do you have the training, experience, and insight to address the problem? Also, they will gauge whether or not they will be able to work with you in partnership. Are you prepared to answer these questions? It's essential to write down the reasons that support your candidacy and your case and for you to practice your pitch about why you are a good fit. I would recommend approaching this with humility. Any signs of arrogance without substance are annoying to funders. Remember, funders are experienced at filtering good ideas from bad ones, and they are always looking to eliminate you from the list of other potentials. Don't let them—have a plan, be prepared, and be humble. You will watch the door open for you, and your ideas will become a reality and change the world.

Summary

The goal of this chapter was to provide you with a sense of the road ahead and the importance of having a plan. It shows how being knowledgeable about the social problem and conducting your pilot provides the preparation for planning. You will better identify your gaps and what you need to do to position yourself for success. Building credibility is critical to solving the problem and becoming the conduit between the funders and the solution. Identify your first funder through common ground and by offering a solution to the social problem directly affecting them. Trust with funders is a vital part of the process, and it takes time to develop. I will talk more about this in the next chapter, "The Art of Fundraising."

Key Lessons

- *Develop a comprehensive business plan backed by credible research and a compelling case study to demonstrate your venture's viability and potential success.*
- *Clearly understand why you are uniquely qualified and well-suited to address the specific problem you have identified, highlighting your expertise, skills, and passion in that area.*
- *Thoroughly research the social problem you aim to solve, gaining in-depth knowledge and insights to build credibility and demonstrate a deep understanding of the issue.*
- *Identify potential gaps or challenges in your planning process and develop strategies to overcome them. Be proactive in addressing obstacles and finding solutions to ensure the smooth execution of your plan.*
- *Cultivate self-confidence in your abilities and the value of your idea. Trust in your research, planning, and preparation, knowing you have thoroughly assessed and believe in the potential of your concept.*

CHAPTER 5

THE ART OF FUNDRAISING

———◆◇◆———

Fundraising is the gentle art of teaching the joy of giving.
—HANK ROSSO

In the depths of my being, I harbored a complex tapestry of beliefs about power, equity, fear, success, and failure. They intertwined within me, shaping my thoughts and emotions. I confronted these mental constructs head-on during a transformative period, daring to question their origins and unravel their hold on me. One thread stood out prominently among the many layers to untangle—my relationship with money. Acknowledging my anxiety over money or scarcity mindset became integral to my healing journey, an essential step to becoming an effective fundraiser. Through this profound process of self-discovery and growth, I realized true transformation begins when we confront the deepest corners of our existence and the barriers that hold us back.

Fundraising Is Your Job as a Leader

Embarking on the journey of starting a charitable organization or social enterprise requires mastering the art of fundraising. This skill can be learned through training and honed with practice. Those who initiate nonprofits and social enterprises often have firsthand experience witnessing the tangible impact their programs have on the communities they serve. This invaluable perspective is a compelling basis for fundraising, as they can passionately convey the stories of transformation and community impact to potential funders.

However, the initial challenge arises: Can you effectively raise funds? Why should funders or donors trust your organization with their resources when established and proven social impact solutions are available? This question plants seeds of self-doubt and negative thoughts, threatening to hinder progress and demoralize your efforts.

I vividly remember feeling out of place and uncomfortable when I first stepped into fundraising. The act of asking for financial support from institutions or private donors was entirely unfamiliar. I faced a daunting challenge that tested my resilience and determination. I didn't realize how ingrained my past relationship with money was; it needed to be changed.

Examine Your Relationship with Money

Growing up in Santa Clara, California, within a low-income household, I was no stranger to my parents' arguments about money. My father frequently expressed frustration over our financial situation, while my mother maintained a more optimistic outlook. However, the constant theme of scarcity and lack left a lasting impression on me. Money always seemed scarce, and every request for money was met with a resounding "no" from my parents. At age ten, my resourceful mother encouraged me to earn money by helping our neighbors with various household tasks. This practice taught me the value of frugality and the importance of saving.

Unfortunately, this upbringing shaped my mentality as I entered adolescence, which led me to adopt a victim mentality. I believed life conspired against me, perpetuating a cycle of scarcity that was difficult to break free from. When I began fundraising for Centro, this scarcity mindset followed me. Recognizing the need for mental and emotional healing, I sought guidance from leaders who could shift my perspective and help me understand money was a tool, not an enemy. I embarked on a journey to change my negative experiences with money into positive ones, slowly unraveling the fears that held me back.

Over five years, with the support of three coaches, I embarked on a profound personal development journey. Xavier Lee, a volunteer executive coach for Centro, invited me to join a mastermind group he co-led with Susan Howard. She was another exceptional executive coach and trainer. Within this group, I recognized how my limiting beliefs about money hindered my ability to raise funds for Centro. The problem was rooted in my self-worth and self-esteem.

More guidance came from Lisa Margulies, a fellow participant in the mastermind group and a financial planner. These experienced coaches and their teachings freed me from old patterns and mental constructs that constrained my fundraising abilities. The coaching process required self-love, forgiveness of myself and my parents, and a commitment to financial literacy. I sought assistance from credit counselors to manage my student loan debt and attended financial literacy classes. Gradually, I regained control over my emotional response to money.

Through my experiences within the mastermind group, I learned a valuable lesson: capital is abundant and flows to where it can be most effectively utilized. This realization liberated me from the illusionary power money once held over me, and I began to move in a new direction of empowerment and abundance.

Understand How Much Money Is Needed

Determining the appropriate amount of funding to ask for is a crucial step before seeking support for your social impact organization. In the upcoming chapter, I will delve deeper into this topic and guide estimating the required funds for implementing your intervention. Initially, I faced several essential questions, such as how many individuals could be trained simultaneously and the projected timeline.

During the early stages of establishing Centro, I required more knowledge about the cost structure involved. However, I needed to understand the value of my time clearly. I accounted for the time required for program activities when developing my initial budget. To gain further insights, I conducted extensive research to address these questions. For instance, I referenced data from reputable organizations like the Aspen Institute, a prominent Washington-based think tank in our industry. This data proved invaluable in estimating our budget and project revenue for the initial years.

According to the data, the national average cost per program participant for providing entrepreneurship education was $4,500 (Klein and Wayman 2008); in 2023, the cost would be $6,300. Utilizing this information, I estimated I could teach approximately twenty to thirty entrepreneurs within a year. Based on these figures, I constructed a budget of $130,000 for program expenses and included an additional 20 percent to account for overhead costs such as rent, office expenses, and insurance.

Whom to Ask for Funding

After developing my estimated budget and establishing a logical explanation for the cost structure based on industry benchmarks, the next challenge in the fundraising process awaited: identifying suitable funding sources. To accomplish this, I thoroughly researched similar organizations to Centro and discovered who the grant funders were. Foundations, corporations, banks, and government agencies consistently emerged as the primary grant funders to nonprofits engaged in economic development, racial equity, and social justice work.

By compiling a comprehensive list of potential funders from other similar organizations to Centro, I created a detailed database on each funder's grant-making process. Before approaching these potential funders for grants, I requested warm introductions from my existing network of professional contacts on LinkedIn and asked them to connect me with program officers. Once granted a meeting with a potential funder, I was prepared to introduce Centro and its programs, learn about their specific grant process, and assess our alignment with their objectives.

Undoubtedly, the ask is the most thrilling aspect of the fundraising process. It is also the most human and emotionally charged part of the interaction. Asking for funding can induce stress due to the fear of rejection, as no one enjoys being turned down. Typically, the ask comes at the end of a standard pitch presentation to a potential funder, following the presentation of who we are, what we do, how we do it, when, and why. It may sound like, "Could we ask for your support to help us transform lives?" or "Would you like to partner with us?" or "Join us in our cause, and together, we will overcome the inequalities in the community." After uttering these words, a heavy silence ensues as we await the potential funder's response. At this moment, my mind races, contemplating the possibility of rejection. Despite knowing that the outcome is not a personal reflection on me as the messenger, the anticipation amplifies the significance of the response.

Fortunately, we could request funding from various sources, including local, state, and federal government entities, family foundations, corporate foundations, individual donors, and other nonprofit foundations. The initial three years were the most challenging as they determined whether we would survive. Through trial and error, I learned from my mistakes, identified my strengths, and became a more effective fundraiser each year because we gained more funders and won more grant funds.

Understand the Facts about Fundraising

Before approaching potential funders for your social impact organization, it is crucial to have several components in place. One essential aspect is psychological preparation, which involves assessing your resilience and readiness to navigate the fundraising journey. It's important to acknowledge that failure and rejection are common experiences in fundraising. Research indicates that, on average, only 10 percent to 30 percent of grant proposals submitted by professional fundraisers are successful. This results in a significant rejection rate. As an early-stage nonprofit, you may face a 90 percent failure rate, or one in ten grant proposals may be accepted and funded (Professional Grant Writer 2021; Lambert 2022). It is a starting point, and there is no shame in it.

There are various reasons behind this high rejection rate. Funders receive many grant proposals, often exceeding their available funds. Additionally, your proposal may not align with their specific portfolio or adhere to their content, format, or length guidelines, resulting in rejection. Furthermore, even if your proposal is a perfect fit, funds may have already been allocated or exceed available funds, which requires waiting for the next grant cycle. Recognizing that these challenges are a normal part of the process is essential. Although overcoming these facts can be difficult, they are integral to developing into an impactful leader of a nonprofit or social enterprise. Learning to manage rejection is a vital aspect of leadership.

When a funder rejects your proposal, it is crucial to understand it is not a personal reflection and should not be taken personally. Managing yourself in the face of a funder's "no" is a skill worth cultivating. Creating a practice, such as a mantra, can be beneficial to reinforce that rejection is not personal. For example, repeating phrases like "Next time" or simply "Next!" can help strengthen resilience when dealing with successful and unsuccessful grant proposals with funders.

Train Others to Fundraise

After years of fundraising, I took the opportunity to train Damanbir Singh, who currently spearheads Centro's grant development and fundraising endeavors. Damanbir's journey with Centro began in 2012 when he joined as a volunteer advisor at the University of San Francisco, where he pursued his MBA. Our paths crossed when I recruited MBA students to become volunteer business advisors for underserved, low-income women entrepreneurs. After dedicating two years of volunteering at Centro, Damanbir expressed his interest in doing more at Centro.

Damanbir says, "One of the toughest parts of the job is when I spend six to seven hours on a grant proposal, submit it, and then the funder returns and says no. I would rather have heard that at the beginning of the process than have spent so much time on a proposal. That's the nature of this work."

Damanbir shares the insight that helped him grow as a professional fundraiser. He says, "It was hard to wrap my head around that I'm going to the funder to ask them for funding and not getting anything in return. I questioned how does this process work? But now, I understand the nature of the work and the sector. I learn new things every day. I'm confident approaching a potential funder and asking them for funding, knowing they receive tax breaks, goodwill, and a form of marketing such as placing their logo on our website. I'm more comfortable asking now than I used to be when I started my fundraising work."

The Long Road to a Funded Budget

Even though I managed to secure an initial grant to fund Centro, I needed to prepare for the challenges that awaited me in securing subsequent grants. The process became increasingly demanding. In 2010, we successfully raised $100,000, but after a year of operation and obtaining our federal nonprofit status the following year, we only managed to raise $18,450. However, in 2012, our efforts yielded $33,000, including contributions of $10,000 from a family foundation, $20,000 from a nonprofit organization, and $3,000 from two financial institutions. Our success rate improved to 15 percent. The turning point came in 2013 when we secured $130,000 in grants from family foundations, financial institutions, and corporate foundations. For the first time, we met our budget, and our success rate soared to 25 percent.

Fast forward to 2023, Centro has raised almost $10 million, with a success rate of nearly 60 percent for new grants and 95 percent for grant renewals. The foundation of our financial stability lies in the renewals, which stem from the close relationships and trust we have built with funders over the years. It is the culmination of relentless hard work. New fundraisers can find their stride and thrive by persevering, proving your organization's worth to funders, establishing trust, and consistently delivering impactful results.

Recipe to Winning

After years of practice, we were praised for the quality of our proposals. We took time to explain our programs effectively, provided our theory of change, and how our mission aligns with the funder's mission. We provide many beneficiary stories of their participation experience in the Centro program and their impact on the community. We make a point to submit error-free and grammatically correct proposals. Before sending any grant proposal, we also present ourselves in person to the potential funder. We have learned that it takes five to seven touchpoints with a potential funder before we would win a grant.

Remember, a well-articulated theory of change is a significant reason professional funding officers will invite you to submit a grant proposal. The theory of change explains how the program services work in the community and create the change you want to see realized. If you make an ambitious transformational effort, the theory of change will be your roadmap to creating the measurable desired future. I will explain this in more detail in the next chapter.

Another critical point is distinguishing between individual donors and institutional, community, family, and corporate foundations. When we started, we didn't have a strong network of high-net-worth donors, so we decided to target family foundations, financial institutions, and corporations instead. These organizations had a process we could easily follow. We had a higher probability of winning grants from these targeted funders than individual donors. Today, we have a proven track record and are a nationally recognized, award-winning nonprofit organization, so we are better positioned to request donations from individuals aligned with our mission. Fundraising takes time to develop. I, unfortunately, didn't know what I didn't know. I didn't have the tools to tell a compelling story about our mission, programs, or impact. We were a new nonprofit organization with an unproven intervention model. We also hadn't conducted an impact study on whether our programs provided a real socioeconomic solution. Although we saw the Centro program beneficiaries learn financial literacy and business skills and transform into new capable business owners, we needed to document the evidence of our impact.

Lack of Racial Equity in Philanthropy

For individuals like me who identify as a person of color, it is important to be aware of the racial biases that philanthropists and investors may harbor. One would assume that well-educated and experienced professionals would be conscious of their biases, but unfortunately, this is not always the case. A research report conducted by Bridgespan and Echoing Green reveals that nonprofit organizations led by people of color receive less grant funding than those led by White leaders (Dorsey, Bradach, and Kim 2020). The report emphasizes the significance of funding leaders of color, as they bring strategies that intimately understand the marginalized experiences of communities of color and their specific challenges. However, this crucial support currently needs to be improved. Jeff Raikes, a cofounder of the Raikes Foundation, adds,

"Philanthropy is overlooking leaders of color who have the most lived experience and understanding of the problems we try to solve" (Dorsey, Bradach, and Kim 2020).The research also highlights a troubling disparity: Black-led organizations, on average, have revenues that are 24 percent lower than their White-led counterparts. The situation becomes even more disheartening when examining unrestricted funding. Black-led organizations have unrestricted net assets that are 76 percent smaller than those of their White-led counterparts. Although not surprising, this disparity is deeply concerning. In the nonprofit sector, the level of unrestricted funding a funder provides is often perceived as a measure of trust or lack thereof in the nonprofit leader (Dorsey, Bradach, and Kim 2022).It is important for individuals who navigate the nonprofit landscape to be aware of these realities and work to change the systemic biases that hinder equitable funding opportunities for leaders of color. Furthermore, it is crucial to acknowledge and address the barriers leaders of color face in securing equitable funding for their nonprofit or social enterprise. According to the research, these barriers include:

1. Limited connections to potential funders: Leaders of color often need more networks and relationships within the philanthropic community to access funding.
2. Challenges in building rapport: Interpersonal biases can hinder the development of trust and relationships with potential funders, placing additional emotional burdens on leaders of color.
3. Difficulties in securing support: Funders may have a limited understanding of culturally relevant approaches, relying on familiar evaluation methods and strategies that may not align with the needs of leaders of color.

4. Sustaining relationships with current funders: Grant renewal processes can be challenging if there is lingering mistrust, and funding decisions may be influenced by a White-centric view of strategic priorities and progress measurement (Dorsey, Bradach, and Kim 2022).

Regardless of these barriers, there are steps you can take to overcome biases and increase your chances of securing funding:

1. Conduct thorough research and preparation: Regardless of your racial background, invest time into researching and planning your approach, including the amount you need, and understand your purpose in serving the community.
2. Share your personal story: Speak from the heart and communicate your experiences. Practice your pitch and storytelling skills to connect with funders on an emotional level effectively.
3. Focus on the problem: Demonstrate a deep understanding of the issue you are addressing, presenting well-researched facts and highlighting the multifaceted impact on the community. Position yourself as an expert solution provider.
4. Be prepared to navigate racial barriers: If you are a person of color, acknowledge the existing racial barriers and equip yourself with the resilience and strength to overcome them.
5. Embrace change and focus on building the future: As Socrates said, *"The secret to change is to focus all of your energy not on fighting the old, but on building the new."* Success will come from your dedication and determination.

By implementing these strategies, you can navigate the funding landscape more effectively and increase your chances of obtaining the necessary resources to make a meaningful impact in your community.

Key Lessons

- **Have patience:** Sometimes, you must wait for the right time before a potential funder says yes. Use this time to keep cultivating the relationship with the funder. Sometimes, it may take years before a funder says yes or invites you to submit a proposal.
- **Relationships are the key:** Fundraising is relationship-driven work. It is important to keep nurturing existing funders' relationships while pursuing new ones. Engagement with funders can be done in various ways, including regular update calls, newsletters, invitations to in-person or virtual events, sending personal notes during holidays, etc.
- **Don't take rejection personally:** While building relationships and grant writing takes time and effort, the funder can still say no to your proposal. Ask for feedback on how you can improve or refine your proposal for the next round, and if there continues to be an alignment with the funder, go for it again.
- **Make sure there is an alignment with the funder's focus area:** Sometimes, a funder has broad areas of focus, for example, economic inclusion or financial literacy. If you are not sure if your work aligns well with what the funder is looking for, don't spend time pursuing the opportunity unless you confirm a good fit exists. If you can't get hold of the program officer, look at their website for past

nonprofits or projects they have supported. Pursue the funder if you see an alignment between what you are proposing and what is on their website (or other research materials you come across—for example, annual reports).

- **Always attempt to schedule an introductory call with a new funder before you send them a grant request:** If you plan to submit a grant request with a new funder, always try to get a call/meeting to introduce yourself and your organization. This increases your chances of securing a grant exponentially with a new funder.

- **If your contact leaves a funding organization, continue building/managing that relationship with the individual:** Fundraising is an intimate sector, and sometimes your contact from one grantor organization might move to another charitable organization. Continue your engagement as your contacts move from one organization to another, as they can help open doors for you with other funders.

- **It's okay to ask for referrals:** If a funder likes your work, it will be easy for them to recommend your organization or send a warm introduction you might need to get to a new funder. Doing your research before making that request and ensuring alignment with the funder's focus areas is essential. To make it easier for the existing funder to make that introduction, have boilerplate items ready— for example, a brief introduction to your organization, impact report, etc., that the funder can share.

- **Don't put all your eggs in one basket:** Always look for opportunities to diversify your revenue sources to ensure financial sustainability. Aim to pursue grants from different funders—for example, financial institutions, corporate foundations, family or community foundations, sponsorships, government, individual donations, or high net-worth individuals. If your nonprofit has a product or service it can offer to the broader community, explore fee-for-service revenue opportunities.

- **Ensure your registrations/statuses are current:** As you submit grant requests, the funder will ask for supporting documents, including current status or other regulatory documents. Always ensure you are in good standing with city, county, and federal agencies that regulate the non-profit organization, and have these documents available when a funder asks. You wouldn't want to miss a grant opportunity because your organization was not in good standing.

- **Have a fundraising strategy:** Don't get carried away with all the grant opportunities you want to pursue. Instead, have a clear strategy that will help you navigate and focus your efforts that yield the best results. Quality proposals that are well-aligned lead to winning grant funds.

- **Finding funders:** I recommend looking at similar organizations as the one you are starting to see who funds them. This was a good start for understanding which donors and grant funders are working toward the same cause.

CHAPTER 6

THE BENEFICIARY, THE INTERVENTION, AND THEORY OF CHANGE

———◆◇◆———

When everyone is included, everyone wins.

—JESSE JACKSON

Observing an industry as an outsider can be a significant advantage. You can see things with fresh eyes and allow your curiosity to lead your creativity to form new possibilities. Before starting Centro, I volunteered for a year at several nonprofits in the community that assisted entrepreneurs. By doing this, I could see how these organizations served their beneficiaries differently.

How these nonprofits executed their program interventions in their community varied as widely as the types of beneficiaries they served. The beneficiaries, or "program participants," ranged in age, educational attainment, socioeconomics, disability, skill level, and gender. My unique experience as a volunteer business advisor provided the perspective I needed to see how nonprofits and beneficiaries work together. From the outsider's view, I saw the gaps clearly, too. Before addressing them, I defined whom I would serve.

Who Is Being Served?

Remembering Adela's profile—woman, immigrant, and low-income—I had parameters I could use as to who would be Centro's beneficiary. Another critical quality to the Centro beneficiary profile would be the need to contribute to building a thriving community by providing quality jobs, products, and services.

Early on, after starting Centro, I met with Antoinette. When I interviewed her as a prospective entrepreneur for the Centro program, she told me, "My obsession with hair began with my little sister. She was a fifth grader looking to feel beautiful on the first day of school, and I was a twelve-year-old with a vision. I found my source of absolute passion and delight—doing hair. My aunt's kitchen soon became the salon of choice for my sister and cousins." Antoinette, an African American woman, dreamed of owning a hair salon in Oakland. She was renting a chair in someone else's salon at the time. She was excited to participate in the Centro program. Meeting Antoinette, I could see she had a presence and grace in her manner and was serious about reaching her entrepreneurial goals. She was a gifted stylist and passionate about making others feel good about themselves with the hairstyles she created for them. She wanted to merge her three loves: hair styling, educating clients about maintaining luscious and healthy hair, and teaching other stylists to be extraordinary hair professionals.

As a program participant, Antoinette faced a major decision if she was to realize her dream. Her volunteer business advisor determined she needed to sell her car to lower her monthly expenses and save money for her business. Unfortunately, she wanted to keep her car. Late one night, two weeks later, as fate would have it, another car slammed into her empty parked car and totaled it. It motivated Antoinette to act, saying, "The universe sent me a clear sign to save money for my boutique salon."

Before becoming an entrepreneur, she had the gumption, enthusiasm, and instinct, but she struggled to convert her vision into a reality. "I knew I wanted to open my salon, but I didn't know how to get started," she says. She met the Centro team while attending the grand opening of her friend's bakery, a Centro program graduate and entrepreneur. She remembered, "As I shook Arturo's hand, I knew my dreams were about to come true." After graduating from the Centro program and saving money for a year, Antoinette started STrUT Oakland Salon. While celebrating the grand opening of Antoinette's new salon, she exclaimed, "I finally achieved my lifelong goal of opening my salon! And the Centro team showed me how." Her business is still open today and going strong.

The beneficiaries served by Centro exhibit the following socioeconomic characteristics and demographics (Centro Community Partners 2022):

- Ninety percent come from low-income backgrounds (earning less than $50,000 per year)
- Eighty percent are female
- Ethnically and racially diverse, including African American (20 percent), Latino (60 percent), Asian (5 percent), Caucasian (5 percent), and Other (10 percent)
- Forty percent are immigrants with English as their second language
- Twenty percent identify as LGBT

Centro's beneficiaries possess many talents. The types of businesses include food products, handcrafts, salons, retail clothing, manufactured goods, professional services, and health and wellness. Moreover, the beneficiaries work full-time at another job while starting their small business. Beneficiaries have an unwavering belief that their new business will help them stabilize their economic life and bring prosperity to their families.

The Change Model

I began to build an intervention model to close the gaps in the economic development system. The gap was that new entrepreneurs were unprepared to receive funding, lacked the knowledge to start their businesses, and faced institutional racism or discrimination. These factors would place them at a disadvantage and result in the need for access to business development services.

Our intervention was to prepare underserved entrepreneurs with a business plan, a leadership development plan, and a credit health improvement plan. After the intervention, they would be ready to partner with capital providers to obtain a microloan. To accomplish this goal, Centro offered an advanced entrepreneurship training program to create plans to start and grow their businesses confidently.

This program required three major components as inputs to the intervention model—the entrepreneur, the volunteer business advisor, and the curriculum. The model would closely resemble what worked for Adela to launch her child daycare business.

First, I recruited entrepreneurs to be the program participants from four different nonprofits, where I volunteered as an advisor. Next, I recruited diverse students from local universities in the Master of Business (MBA) programs to become volunteer business advisors to the entrepreneurs in the program. They would partner with the entrepreneurs to create the deliverables and complete the Centro entrepreneurship program. Fortunately, seven entrepreneurs agreed to be a part of the first cohort. Lastly, I searched for an entrepreneurship training curriculum for my target population. Unfortunately, none were a relevant fit to the requirements we needed. Therefore, I created our program curriculum.

Each component of the intervention change model had to be tested to see if it worked. I had my fingers crossed.

Testing the Intervention

The pilot cohort would complete the fourteen-week Entrepreneur Readiness Program. Each team would be challenged to reach critical milestones. At the end of the program, each team delivered a business plan with financials, a leadership development plan, a credit improvement plan, and a final presentation. I taught the entrepreneurs business lessons on Wednesday nights and trained the MBAs to be advisors on Friday nights.

With each passing week, I could see the positive transformation for entrepreneurs and business advisors. At the program's start, entrepreneurs were shy to share their stories and slowly opened up about their talents to other entrepreneurs in the cohort. By contrast, the business advisors came from privileged backgrounds and were well-educated, confident, and analytical in their abilities. As we approached the end of the program, sentiments and attitudes shifted and changed.

By the end of the fourteen weeks, the entrepreneurs could confidently present their ideas and think critically about their business models. They formed strong bonds with each other and deepened their trust among the entrepreneurs in the cohort. They refined the quality of their products and services and found new ways to reach their customers. The entrepreneurs learned how to use financial tools to measure their new business key performance metrics. They increased their credit score so that they could access a microloan. They improved their self-confidence and self-esteem and were ready to execute their plans. Although technically savvy, the volunteer MBA student business advisors learned to examine a real business problem and practiced developing creative solutions to assist their entrepreneurs. They learned about the gravity of their business advice to the entrepreneur, so there was little room for error. Advisors became more aware of their social biases and privilege. As a result of rolling up their sleeves and working alongside the entrepreneurs, they understood the difficulty of starting a business, how to be effective advisors, and the risks they needed to manage. They became more emotionally intelligent, humble, and empathetic listeners.

Five of the seven entrepreneurs who started the Centro pilot program finished and graduated. Two entrepreneurs dropped out of the program due to family and health issues. Three teams were funded in the first cohort, and the other two teams self-funded. In the second cohort, twelve teams started, and ten teams finished the program. I was delighted by the results. Our program empowered entrepreneurs to realize their dreams of becoming small business owners, helping create more social justice and racial equity in the community. However, upon review, we found that our intervention model had some significant issues that prevented it from becoming sustainable.

After guiding entrepreneurs to start and grow their businesses repeatedly for several years, Centro could identify specific patterns that would emerge among the cohorts. They became recognizable roadmaps with measurable results. Successful entrepreneurs who reached their milestones and achieved their goals left a trail of measurable evidence behind them.

This evidence was documented and measured, becoming the feedback loop reinforcing and modifying the Centro change model. Such evidence was the amount of time the volunteer

MBA and entrepreneur would spend working on the new business. For example, if advisors spent more than one hundred hours in the fourteen-week program, the entrepreneur would graduate from the program and launch a new business. Another indicator was that when entrepreneurs tested their products in public venues, they had higher rates of success than those entrepreneurs who did not.

Another example is the entrepreneurs who examined their personal finances and credit reports and developed financial literacy skills leading to greater self-awareness. It became the step-by-step process in our curriculum that entrepreneurs used to build their skills, abilities, and confidence. As they moved through the steps, they obtained the necessary resources, such as capital and support services, and started their small business.

Theory of Change

For any social intervention model, you must determine its components and how to use them to measure results. Did the intervention make a difference? What is the evidence? Could the evidence be measured? Transformational change takes time to measure the results of the intervention's impact.

Each step in the entrepreneur's journey is part of the "Theory of Change" (ToC). According to the Fund against Child Labour, a ToC links the relationship between the inputs, the intervention, and the measurable desired results. It has the following components:

Component	Context
The Problem Statement	What social or environmental problem needs to be solved?
Context	The situation in which the program/project occurs.
Inputs	What we use. The resources required for a project or program.
Activities	What we do. These are activities in the lesson plans.
Outputs	What we produce. Outputs are the tangible products as a result of the activities.
Outcomes	What we achieve. Outcomes are the behavioral changes that result from the project outputs.
Impacts	Why we do it. Long-term changes are the results that derive from an accumulation of outcomes.
Assumptions	What are the necessary conditions for change, or the "underlying conditions or resources that need to exist for planned change to occur?"
Risks	Potential impacts of the program that may undermine its success.

Source: (Fund against Child Labour 2018)

The following flow chart shows the Theory of Change Model:

Source: (Poverty Action 2016)

The Problem Statement

The problem statement should be clear and concise. It provides a legitimate perspective of the social problem identified and creditable reference sources. The following is Centro's problem statement:

Women and minorities have emerged as the fastest-growing segments of new business creation in the US. Yet they face greater barriers due to institutional racism, such as limited access to enterprise-building tools and capital, which impede growth, thus denying them the opportunity to create an asset-building enterprise as means of financial stability (Barr 2015). About 13 million small business owners are women, and 6.5 million are women of color (American Express 2019). However, women only receive 16 percent of small business loans and 4 percent of the total dollar value of loans (Cantwell 2014).

The statement identifies the affected population, the social issue or problem challenging the population, its magnitude, and the credible sources. The target populations are women and minorities, and its magnitude is thirteen million small businesses. The problem is institutional racism and bias, the lack of access to capital, and enterprise-building educational resources.

A critical component for leaders is to have the social issue documented and observed by credible sources. Why is this important to show in the problem statement? The answer is that funders, investors, and supporters will believe you only if your observations are sourced and documented by credible observers (i.e., by a trained researcher or scientist) who specialize in science, social, economic, or environmental issues.

The Intervention—Inputs & Activities

As mentioned, our ToC includes in its inputs: the low-income entrepreneur, the volunteer MBA student advisor, the entrepreneurship education and leadership training curriculum, a training room, and the program facilitator.

Next, we identify the activities (what we do) to create the change we want to see occur with the entrepreneurs. The activities are the intervention and become the program the beneficiaries participate in and complete. The program helps the low-income women entrepreneur transition from her current state of economic instability to a more economically and self-sustaining stable state.

Centro's ToC activities involve developing new skills, abilities, and mindsets. The foundation is formed by participating in business planning to exercise and practice the formation of critical thinking and analytical mental processes. These activities include learning the basics of several business areas, such as strategy, business finance, marketing, product/service development, and personal budgeting. Other activities in the program include working with other entrepreneurs in the cohort that target building an entrepreneur's growth mindset, self-confidence, and self-esteem. This helps them manage their fear of failure, self-doubt, and limiting beliefs and keeps them moving forward. The entrepreneur learns management, teamwork, and communication skills by working with the volunteer business advisor leading to greater confidence.

The Outputs & Outcomes

Envisioning the future desired state is critical so that the intervention leads beneficiaries to the target. What was created in the intervention? Can the change be measured in the beneficiary's behavior? To help answer these questions, we can use the following two components of the ToC: the outputs and outcomes.

Outputs (what we produced) are the results or deliverables created by the activities in the intervention. In the Centro change model, the outputs each team created were a business plan, financial plan, leadership development plan, credit improvement plan, and final presentation. These outputs were carefully designed and related to the outcomes entrepreneurs developed in the intervention program.

Outcomes (what we achieved) are the desired future state, such as new behavior in the entrepreneur. There were several significant behavior changes in entrepreneurs. They started their small business, improved their finances, increased their credit scores, and accessed microloans. Their confidence, empowerment, critical thinking skills, and self-esteem increased.

The Impact

What is the lasting impact to be seen in the community? An impact is a positive and sustained change in the social issue being addressed or solved. By observing the results of the outputs and outcomes, we can start to understand the long-term effects of the intervention program. The accumulation of outcomes creates the impact and the desired future state: increase the number of low-income women of color who start and grow their small businesses, reach financial stability, and overcome the challenges of discrimination and systemic racism.

Measurement & Feedback Loop

Let's take a closer look at impact by collecting data to measure changes. We collect data at several points in the beneficiary's intervention or entrepreneurship journey. Baseline information is collected at registration and throughout the program, at graduation, then six months after graduation, and one year hence.

Upon program completion, survey tools are used to collect essential beneficiary data. The data is gathered through one-on-one interviews and survey questionnaires. One of the tools we use is the Net Promoter Score, which measures the satisfaction and loyalty levels among the beneficiaries after they complete our programs. By asking the beneficiaries why they chose the survey score, we can use their feedback to help us understand and improve our interventions (Net Promoter System 2023).

Other methods are survey questions that explore what the entrepreneur was able to learn, such as changes to their understanding of business and financial literacy concepts and steps to start a business. After twelve months of completing the program, two long-term surveys are implemented to measure the growth of an entrepreneur's business, retention and application of the information they learned at Centro, and other impacts on their lives and communities. There is an assessment of whether the entrepreneurs have accessed capital, hired employees, increased their savings, and other measures of the economic strength of a business and community. Keeping the beneficiaries engaged with Centro throughout the year is critical so they have continuous support services. We offer ongoing coaching services to our entrepreneurs throughout this crucial period.

This data-gathering process allows program participants or beneficiaries to actively partner with us to provide accurate data about what changed after the intervention. It also requires tracking beneficiaries after the program for years to keep accumulating the necessary data.

The Model Assumptions

The ToC assumptions may include philosophies, principles, values, and how the program will be executed in the community being served. The ToC's assumptions at Centro assumed the beneficiary could commit their time and energy to learn new skills and knowledge. There was an expectation that the entrepreneur was open and willing to change. Another assumption was beneficiaries could learn new skills and abilities in three months. Beneficiaries met weekly for two to three hours for in-person sessions. This didn't include time with their business advisor outside the classroom, which could be between eighty to one hundred hours. However, the time required to learn the new business knowledge and skills needed to start a business was about thirty hours of in-classroom sessions plus the time the entrepreneur spent with their business advisor over a period of fourteen weeks.

Summary

This chapter focuses on the following questions: Who is your customer or beneficiary? What is the intervention model going to be? What are you going to measure? What is the impact?

Understanding the uniqueness of your beneficiary is key. Focusing on their specific socioeconomic characteristics, learning differences, and ability to change will help you design a customized intervention model.

Transformation change is challenging to measure since it requires frequent data collection over long periods. This data needs to be analyzed to see if any patterns emerge. More difficult is measuring the personal transformation that happens to the beneficiaries. This requires robust surveys and personal interviews to collect the appropriate data consistently. Feedback loops provide beneficiary data results that help inform the outputs and outcomes funders and donors look for in an intervention program serving the community. The major obstacle as a leader is making the intervention cost-effective, scalable, and impactful.

The ToC is critical to developing and sustaining an intervention strategy. Creating interdependence between the strategy and the desired outcomes to make social change a reality is a part of developing a robust theory of change. The bottom line is how well the intervention creates a fundamental change in the beneficiary's preparedness to reach their goal and how it will be measured.

Key Lessons

The Beneficiary

- *Understand who your beneficiary is.*
- *Take the time to understand the services your beneficiary needs.*
- *Identify the socioeconomics of your beneficiary.*

- List the barriers for your beneficiaries, such as digital literacy, technology, education attainment, and learning styles.
- Document the personal stories of your beneficiaries and share them with your team, funders, and supporters.

The Theory of Change

- Begin with the problem statement, followed by your change model that maps the inputs, activities, outputs, outcomes, and impact.
- It aims to define how strategies and actions will achieve change, communicate the vision for this change, and identify the expected results.
- Using a theory of change map helps to visualize the pathway of change. Outcomes can be "mapped" in a linear or causal sequence.
- Recognize that outcomes may result from single or multiple strategies. The intervention strategies may lead to common goals.
- Link strategies to outcomes and goals. This process helps the strategy lead to an expected outcome. Most change strategies include high interdependency among strategies and outcomes since it takes more than one strategy to influence particular outcomes.

CHAPTER 7

SPARK OF INNOVATION

———◆◇◆———

The best way to predict the future is to create it.
—PETER F. DRUCKER

Have you experienced a transformative moment that ignited your passion and opened doors to new possibilities? A moment so powerful it took your breath away and opened your eyes to a new world? On a Saturday in June of 2011, I attended the Latinos in Social Media conference at the Computer History Museum in Mountain View, California. As I walked into the room filled with excitement and anticipation, little did I know this event would mark the beginning of a remarkable journey. At that time, I was a novice in the world of social media, having recently opened a Facebook account. I kept it a secret to myself, unaware of social media's immense impact and potential. But that day, as I immersed myself in the vibrant atmosphere of the conference, a hidden passion within me ignited, and my perspective of the world was forever changed.

There were six of us seated at a round table, and we started introducing ourselves. I heard many of them talk about their experience in social media and why they were at this conference. I remember I was the only one from the nonprofit industry, and this was my first conference representing Centro Community Partners as its founder. Since I have the word "partners" in the title of our company's name written on my name tag, many at the table assumed I was a venture capitalist. This was funny because it kept happening in the line for lunch, in the men's restroom, and during cocktail hour. Each time, I explained I was with a nonprofit educational organization, and we taught entrepreneurship.

Study Trends to Guide Your Social Innovation

As I settled into my seat, the presentation got underway. I was hooked. We were presented with the latest technologies trends and the presenters' five- to ten-year predictions that connected to social media platforms. I was blown away by how fast the adoption rates of smartphones doubled each year. Everyone on earth would own at least one smartphone but not a computer. This fact hit me hard! Another insight was the number of apps being created at a rate of 1,000 per week. In 2011 there were about 328,000 apps in the app store, which was expected to grow to more than three million (Lawson 2010). More growth was projected in the number of social media users, increasing from around one billion to more than three billion. The fact that everyone would have a smartphone was a game changer for every industry.

These trends would change educational nonprofits too. A few years earlier, a professor with the Peter F. Drucker School of

Management in Claremont, California, taught me to watch global trends to understand more considerable societal changes in politics and the economy. That professor was Peter F. Drucker himself. He also mentored me. Drucker's writings contributed to the philosophical and practical foundations of knowledge workers, modern business corporations, non-profits, and governments in the twentieth century.

Drucker taught me, "Innovation is change that creates a new dimension of performance" and "The truly important events on the outside are not the trends. They are changes in the trends. These determine the success or failure of an organization and its efforts." Drucker was right. As a leader, I needed to be mindful of the implication of technology trends to teach entrepreneurship in a way that was impossible before. It could be used in innovative ways.

Epiphany! Everything we taught at Centro—entrepreneurship education, business planning, and leadership skills—could be integrated into a mobile app. It would be scalable and directly reach our target community. Inspired, I started to draw on a napkin the different areas of how the app could function. I saw the future at that moment. One of the other guests at the table noticed me as I raced to get my thoughts on paper. She said, "Hey Arturo, what are you drawing?" I said politely with a grin, "Our future is an app to bring entrepreneurship education to everyone!" We both laughed. But it was true. I was inspired by the trends presented at the conference. I would not stop thinking about what we needed to do next at Centro—creating an innovative, mobile, technology-enabled, and educational nonprofit changed everything.

Innovation as a Solution

Why was developing an innovative solution for the economic development industry essential? The industry needed a scalable platform to provide access to entrepreneurship education, business planning, coaching, and capital. Furthermore, a technology-enabled teaching tool would help to significantly reduce the cost of training an entrepreneur in business planning. In 2011, underserved low-income entrepreneurs in the San Francisco Bay Area could not readily access affordable entrepreneurship education, capital, or mentorship. You paid a fee for a community-based nonprofit or community college class.

According to research by the Aspen Institute, the most significant challenge for microenterprise development organizations (MDOs) like Centro is the costs associated with entrepreneurship education. This includes the high cost per entrepreneur (i.e., $4,500 was the national average per entrepreneur) and access to business advisory services (Aspen Institute 2014). For example, an entrepreneurship workshop series of twenty-five to thirty hours for ten entrepreneurs costs an average of $45,000 for the MDO. The high costs limited many aspiring low-income entrepreneurs from being served because it could not be scaled at that cost average. Therefore, MDOs struggled to scale their entrepreneurship programs and limited their offerings to the community.

The Innovation Dream Team

The Monday after the social media conference, my team, including MBA student interns Kathyrn Sobondy, Darius

Mahajer, and one of our professional advisors, Naldo Peliks, worked in our tiny office. I was so excited to talk with them about what I saw at the conference and told them Centro had to put everything we could on a mobile app. They looked at each other, then at me, and laughed out loud. One said, "But Centro doesn't even have a website." Followed by more laughing. My novel idea was amusing and unrealistic to them. My team was laughing at me! At that moment, I knew I was on to something big. It didn't hurt my feelings because I was sure about the idea. Although it sounded unbelievable, I saw the future in that moment of inspiration drawn on the napkin at the conference. It was going to happen! The question was how.

After the chuckles died down, Naldo showed more curiosity and asked questions about what I meant. Naldo was tech-savvy and joined Centro in the fall of 2010 as a part-time volunteer. He helped me manage the MBA student volunteer advisors working with the entrepreneurs in the Entrepreneurship Readiness Program. I asked him how we could use a mobile app to help us teach entrepreneurship and scale. Naldo said, "I don't know, but I don't see why not." Naldo became the first believer, and he started working on building the prototype.

Naldo—perfect for this challenge—became the architect to operationalize our programs and my vision into a tangible technology-based service. He created an innovation lab at Centro. His brilliance was designing short experiments and testing how we would produce practical curriculum and learning tools to help entrepreneurs learn business concepts. His philosophical approach would become the foundation of our operations, including the processes and procedures of how we did everything at Centro in the early years. Naldo introduced human-centered design concepts, rapid prototyping, and minimal viable product development processes.

Human-centered design is an approach to problem-solving commonly used in management and engineering wire frameworks that develop solutions to problems by involving the human perspective in all steps of the problem-solving process (Landry 2020). Rapid prototyping and a minimum viable product, or MVP, is a product with enough features to attract early-adopter customers and validate a product idea early in the product development cycle, which then provides feedback for product development in rapid cycles (Product Plan 2023).

Naldo proved himself a real asset earlier on as a volunteer for Centro. He was from San Francisco and studied at the University of San Francisco. He had technology experience before earning his MBA at Instituto de Empresa (IE) Business School in Madrid, Spain. He also spoke several languages fluently, including Japanese, Portuguese, Spanish, and English. His practical and realistic view of the world grounded me, and his even-keeled disposition allowed for many level-headed discussions. We met at a mutual friend's home for a party in San Francisco. Once Naldo and I were introduced, we clicked and started sharing experiences and ideas. I talked about Centro; he spoke about his MBA experience and living in Spain.

In 2012, our innovation team needed someone who knew about adult learning and could help us with prototyping. I told Naldo I had the perfect person in mind.

In 2009, I met a most interesting person named Daniel John (DJ) Healy while in line to get our books signed by an author in Claremont, California. I introduced myself to DJ and learned he was an MBA student at the Drucker School, originally from Wyoming. He studied international relations at the University of Colorado in Boulder and was interested in international development and diplomacy. DJ was also fluent in Russian and in the Peace Corps teaching English as a Second Language (ESL) in Georgia, in Eastern Europe. DJ relocated to San Francisco, so we asked him to join us at Centro. DJ's abilities and novel way of thinking about adult teaching complemented Naldo's talent for operationalizing new ideas, and together, they would be a powerful combination.

Forming a team of people with whom the leader aligns several shared values is critical. Fortunately, Naldo, DJ, and I had values that aligned and complemented working together. Our mission was to innovate and create something new, so our shared values guided the decisions throughout the process. We yielded results by overcoming failures and achieving small successes.

The Path of Innovation

Innovation is a series of successes and failures. There is no way around that fact. By combining the team's knowledge of entrepreneurship, adult education modalities, and mobile technology, we were on our way to building the prototype of a cost-effective, scalable mobile app for economic development. This would make it possible to standardize entrepreneurship education and give access to anybody anywhere with a smartphone. But first, we changed the way we taught entrepreneurship.

Our path of innovation was not technology-based at first. We instead needed to take baby steps and examine how teaching entrepreneurship could be changed. Centro used the traditional classroom instruction method in which the instructor or teacher would lead the lesson providing guidance and information to students (this is one-directional learning). This model relies on the experience of the instructor or teacher, which creates a limiting factor to scaling.

When DJ joined the team, he challenged us by saying, "Let's flip the classroom instead of utilizing one-directional learning." I didn't know what he meant. DJ explained that the "flipped classroom" approach aims to increase student engagement and learning by having students complete their readings at home and work on live problem-solving during class time. It promotes critical thinking and effective use of classroom time and places more responsibility for learning on the student. In addition to the "flipped classroom" approach, DJ wanted to integrate the ESL methodology into Centro's curriculum because he saw it could make the classroom experience more interactive and go beyond Centro's one-directional teaching. Using ESL practices such as communicative language teaching (CLT), which emphasizes the student's ability to communicate in real-life contexts, we made entrepreneurship education more practical than theoretical. ESL allowed students to learn to make requests, accept offers, explain things, and express their feelings and preferences. Inspired, I put DJ in charge of Centro's curriculum development, teaching, and entrepreneurship facilitation.

Using the ESL methodology in an entrepreneurship training context was brilliant and strategic. We figured out how to get past the old traditional method of teaching entrepreneurship and hit upon the idea of merging two different teaching methods—the "flipped classroom" and the ESL methodology. Instead of lectures and presentations to the entrepreneurs in the one-directional traditional method, we would have entrepreneurs do a series of engaging activities. For example, these activities included selecting and prioritizing their values into a shortlist and exploring how they would guide their business decision-making. This was the next evolutionary step that would allow us to make a curriculum that could adapt to mobile technology.

The activities needed to be more engaging. Naldo and DJ created new preclass activities and slowly figured out what worked best with the participants. Once the team had functioning preclass paper exercises, we moved forward to engineer and code it into a prototype. At this point, we brought in Silvio, an app developer and engineer from Venezuela. He coded the prototype of the Centro app for the iPhone.

In the summer of 2013, Naldo, Silvio, and DJ created more preclass exercises and converted them into the beta version of the Business Planning App with thirty activities. Although the team created a functional interface for the user to complete the activities, the app had challenges and drawbacks.

The Centro's Innovation Pathway is shown as follows.

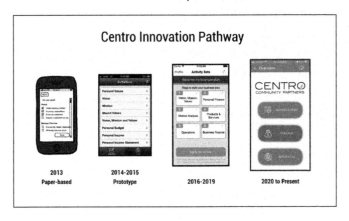

Image source: Centro Community Partners 2022, "Our Innovation Pathway."

DJ recounts the experience, "There were so many steps in automating the business plan that we didn't get to a final version. But at this point, we needed to try another approach. We started to look at how we problem-solve to see if it made sense. Before, we would try, and if it worked, we would move on, but if it didn't, we also moved on to another problem. It wasn't until we read the book *The Lean Startup* that I think things clicked. Here was a book about what we were doing. That brought more structure to our innovation approach at Centro." The critical element at the core of the *Lean Startup* methodology was the build-measure-learn feedback loop. This loop helped us figure out the problem that needed to be solved and then led us to develop a minimal viable product (MVP) to begin learning as quickly as possible. This would involve measuring and learning to include actionable metrics demonstrating cause-and-effect questions.

The prototype was called the Business Planning Tool (BPT) and was completed in early 2014. The BPT walked entrepreneurs through a series of engaging and interactive activities that would create a business plan. A curriculum was explicitly designed to complement the BPT and help entrepreneurs learn to think critically and develop their business models. Our app used simple terminology, assuming entrepreneurs had no formal business training or knowledge.

Prototype Field Testing

We initially tested the prototype with a pilot group of merchants in the low-income neighborhood of the Fruitvale District of Oakland. DJ remembered, "I ran all over the Fruitvale District (Oakland's Latino neighborhood). None of the entrepreneurs in the first test cohort could download the Centro app. Instead, we gave them donated iPhones and walked them through the app because nobody could figure out how to use the Centro app on their own. It was a big challenge, but we also loved it. We were learning things fast and making corrections."

We saw positive results once we got the test cohort running the app. Centro realized a 40 percent reduction in classroom training costs and an 80 percent reduction in time spent on individualized assistance compared to the previous year with no mobile technology. With these results and additional positive feedback from other entrepreneurs and community partners, our assumptions were validated, and we decided to push forward with further app development.

Integration of Centro App

Once the beta version of the business planning app was on the iPhones, we could apply it to our programs. We were experimenting with incorporating the technology app tool into an entrepreneur's educational journey. We created the foundation of the Centro entrepreneurship educational programs.

As a result of combining the technology-based Centro app with the business plan activities and the two teaching methods, we created new programs, such as the Bootcamp and the Basic Entrepreneurship Program. These programs became our scalable solution that would be effective and cost-efficient in English, Spanish, and Portuguese.

Moving an Industry Forward

Centro is unique in the economic development industry. It innovated in two areas—utilizing mobile app technology as an entrepreneurship training tool, and the "flipped classroom" method used to teach adults. Efficiency and impact were the results. Centro brought down the cost of entrepreneurship training from $4,500 to about $1,000 per entrepreneur in a program and $200 per entrepreneur who completes the app independently without the Centro program. Entrepreneurs like Adela would now only have to download the Centro app and complete the fun activities over two to three hours to complete their business plan in Spanish, compared to the months it took Adela initially.

Centro uses its mobile app technology as a virtual hub to make accessible business planning, microloans, and other small business development services offered by an ecosystem of nonprofits focusing on microenterprise development. This app helped to create efficiencies, standardize quality, and make learning fun and engaging for entrepreneurs.

Today, the Centro app (Centro Business Planning Tool) is free on iOS (Apple) and Android devices. We continue introducing new functionality that automatically generates business plans in multiple languages for the entrepreneur and provides access to microloans and other nonprofit business resources. As of January 2023, the Centro app has been downloaded in over one hundred countries and translated into several languages, including English, Spanish, Portuguese, Russian, Chinese, and Cambodian Khmer.

Centro's App Acknowledgments and Awards for Innovation & Impact

- *2015 – GOOGLE IMPACT CHALLENGE: BAY AREA FINALISTS*
- *2016 – DRUCKER PRIZE FINALIST*
- *2018 – NBC UNIVERSAL FOUNDATION PROJECT INNOVATION WINNER*
- *2020 – THE WORKERS LAB FINALISTS*
- *2021 – MIT SOLVE WINNER - REIMAGINING PATHWAYS TO EMPLOYMENT IN THE US CHALLENGE*
- *2021 – NATIONAL AARP PURPOSE PRIZE WINNER*
- *2022 – PROGRESS MAKERS NATIONAL AWARD WINNER CITI FOUNDATION*

Summary

Do not be afraid of trying something new, regardless of how ridiculous it may seem. Instead, forge ahead and let curiosity and the love of learning lead the way. Only some people are going to believe in your innovative idea or approach. That is okay. Most will see the future differently than you do. Just keep moving forward and build it so it can be tested because you owe it to yourself to see what could be created.

Remember that the best way to innovate is to understand what problem you are trying to solve. We looked at the problem from different perspectives to teach entrepreneurship differently because the old traditional methods were slow, nonscalable, and expensive. Using methodologies from other areas can be applied to solve your social problem. Our entrepreneurship training program became more dynamic, scalable, and cost-effective by incorporating ESL methods, the "flipped classroom" theory, and *Lean Startup* strategies.

Key Lessons

- *Embrace a mindset of openness to change and a drive to innovate, as this is the fertile ground where creativity flourishes.*
- *Surround yourself with individuals who believe in your vision and are willing to contribute to innovation, building a team of passionate supporters.*
- *Seek out teammates who possess complementary skills and share your values, as their diverse perspectives will enhance the creative and innovative potential of the group.*

- *Engage in constructive discourse and debate with your teammates, which is essential for exploring possibilities and determining viable ideas. Through this process, generate and test ideas to create robust and promising solutions that can thrive and drive innovation.*
- *Recognize that we all have blind spots and areas where we may be unaware of potential challenges or limitations. Addressing these blind spots is crucial to fostering a more comprehensive, practical, and effective approach to innovation.*

CHAPTER 8

CHANGE THE WORLD

———◆◇◆———

Faith is taking the first step even when you don't see the whole staircase.

—DR. MARTIN LUTHER KING, JR.

Changing the world for the better requires truth, conviction, and a willingness to step into the unknown. Embarking on a new journey brings excitement and uncertainty, demanding courage and faith in oneself. One crucial aspect is to know and believe in your truth. It is essential not to be discouraged by the failures of others but instead to listen to your truth and embrace your uniqueness. For example, I faced challenges with dyslexia and held a strong value for social justice, which shaped my perspective.

Along the journey, you will discover your superpowers and inner strength, which will transform and enhance your abilities. Even if the end goal is unclear, it's essential to keep moving forward. You are on the right path if you serve others needing your expertise.

Passion plays a vital role in social impact work. If you don't have a genuine passion for the cause you want to pursue, it is recommended not to engage in it. Passion is an inexhaustible source of motivation, driving you to accomplish even the most challenging tasks. However, it is unconditional love that truly makes an impact. The effects of inequities and discrimination in my life compelled me to do community work aligned with my social justice values.

Use love as a powerful force to help you accomplish social change goals. It sustains you through challenging times and helps you overcome your setbacks. You can impact the world meaningfully by channeling your passion and love into your work.

Bust Out of Your Bubble

If you aspire to bring about meaningful change, delving deeply into the social problem you wish to address is crucial. Stepping outside your comfort zone and visiting other countries provides invaluable perspectives and insights. By exploring different communities and their solutions to similar social problems, you may discover relevant and practical approaches that can be adapted to your context.

I am fortunate for the opportunity to have visited over thirty countries in Africa, Asia, Europe, and Latin America throughout my work and studies. Whether as a student, winemaker, management consultant, or senior economic advisor, each role allowed me to examine the same socioeconomic problem from various angles. These experiences have played a significant role in shaping my character, professional acumen, and leadership style. Learning from countless mistakes, failures, and misfortunes instilled a sense of humility, which remains my greatest teacher. Furthermore, my love and faith in God are guiding forces, providing inspiration, courage, and fortitude to carry out the necessary work in social justice and community development.

For instance, during my time as a senior advisor to the United States Agency for International Development (USAID) in the Development Credit Authority and at Grameen Foundation, I visited several countries, including Angola, Colombia, Guatemala, India, Mexico, Nigeria, Peru, South Sudan, and Tanzania. These visits shed light on the importance of entrepreneurship education and access to capital in countries grappling with concentrated poverty. Governments in these nations recognized the need to support communities in creating small businesses to combat poverty.

Witnessing firsthand the stark realities of poverty and its impact on people's lives, especially children facing malnutrition and lack of necessities, deeply affected me. It was truly heartbreaking. The experience reinforced the realization that there is a long road ahead in eradicating poverty from the world. However, it also served as an enriching experience that informed my efforts in creating more effective solutions and programs at Centro.

By immersing oneself in different communities and learning from their challenges and successes, one can gain a broader perspective and contribute to finding innovative solutions to social problems.

For instance, among the fifty states in the US, the average poverty rate is 11.4 percent or thirty-seven million, with the highest level in Mississippi at 19.6 percent and the lowest rate in New Hampshire at 7.3 percent (Center for American Progress 2020). Although overall poverty has decreased in the last thirty years, recent reports show the US poverty rate to have increased again due to income inequality, inflation, poor education, unemployment, and personal debt. Access to education, access to entrepreneurship resources, access to jobs, and access to financial literacy would help to alleviate poverty (US Census Bureau 2022). Centro provides the path for everyone to use entrepreneurship as a means out of poverty and a way to create financial stability.

Break Down Assumptions

You must challenge existing assumptions and paradigms if you want to create change. Before you change any system, you must examine why people think the way they do. What are the assumptions that hold the current system in place? These assumptions usually need to be corrected, adding another layer of complexity to the social problem. So as a leader, it is up to you to break these assumptions down by presenting a new perspective that can lead to a solution to be tested.

The assumptions in the economic development systems:

1) To provide effective entrepreneurship training, trainers must have extensive entrepreneurship experience and business education. In other words, costly experts are needed to teach.

2) Entrepreneurship training programs can't be standardized because they need to be adapted to the specific needs of the entrepreneur, which vary due to location, industry, business type, and background.

3) Mobile technology is an ineffective channel for delivering entrepreneurship training and business planning support to low-income entrepreneurs because they will be intimidated by the technology and won't have access to it.

For years, these assumptions prevented the development of scalable entrepreneurship education and training for low-income entrepreneurs across the industry. Determined to break down these assumptions, Centro uniquely positioned itself to solve this problem through innovative processes, testing, failing, succeeding, and repeating the cycle. Our tenacity paid off. We created scalable access to entrepreneurship education and capital by inventing new cost-effective ways to integrate training with mobile technology to reach our community entrepreneurs in more than one hundred countries. We hope to help more organizations provide low-income entrepreneurs with educational resources and technology that is effective, affordable, and accessible.

Driving Social Change

After starting Centro, we were able to help many entrepreneurs and communities. Centro has served over 8,000 women and minority entrepreneurs, providing valuable support and facilitating access to over $6.3 million in loans and grants. Centro makes a substantial impact on economic mobility and inclusion through its efforts by offering more than 13,300 hours of one-on-one business advisory services to underserved entrepreneurs.

Centro plays a pivotal role in helping entrepreneurs transform their ideas into thriving businesses, enabling them to achieve financial independence over time. Entrepreneurs turn to Centro because they have dreams and aspirations that need guidance and nurturing. The team assists them on their journey, helping them tap into their limitless creativity and aspire to a greater vision of themselves. This process involves working with entrepreneurs through their most challenging periods of self-discovery as they progress from idea conception to becoming self-determined and self-actualizing business owners.

One key aspect defining Centro's mission is its commitment to racial equity and social justice. We purposefully identify these goals as central to their community empowerment work. The communities served have historically experienced neglect, lack of resources, and generations of systemic racism, leading to underlying health conditions and economic exclusion. Centro aims to break the cycles of poverty by providing support to individuals and communities with limited or no access to resources and capital.

To drive socioeconomic change, Centro offers a range of programs and services focused on entrepreneurship education, financial literacy, and leadership development for low-income, minority, and women entrepreneurs. By providing culturally and linguistically relevant resources, information, and financial tools, Centro ignites the imagination and will of low-income women and entrepreneurs of color, empowering them to break the cycle of poverty through their entrepreneurial spirit.

We continuously evolve our approach by incorporating the community's voice, addressing their needs, and analyzing data collected annually. We leverage technology and adopt leading programmatic practices to generate sustained community impact. Our efforts aim to catalyze economic development, foster systemic change, create jobs, and alleviate poverty.

Centro brings about transformative changes in the lives of entrepreneurs and communities, working for a more equitable and just society through entrepreneurship, economic empowerment, and community development initiatives.

Centro's Impact Highlights

According to our *October 2022 Impact Report*, the Centro program's sample size of 372 entrepreneur graduates showed the following progress (Centro Community Partners 2022):

- Fifty-four percent are in the concept stage, but 59 percent of the graduates reported having started their businesses.
- Thirty-one percent started paying themselves.
- Twenty percent hired staff.

Annual Sales
- Of the entrepreneurs who graduated more than one year ago, 73 percent reported having sales, generating a total annual revenue of $11 million and an average annual revenue of $58,627.

Investment in Jobs
- Of those with sales, 71 percent incurred labor costs over the last twelve months, resulting in $3,859,000 in total labor costs and an average of $28,500 per business.

Access to Capital
- Twenty-eight percent of the entrepreneurs reported having accessed capital within the last two years, representing $1,238,000.

Testimonials
- Centro App
  - "I love that it is so easy to use and straightforward. The app helped me create my business plan with ease. The vision and values part of the app made me rethink my purpose for this business. I love that the app is easy to use and asks all the right questions to create a complete business plan. Overall, it is a great tool."
  - "I enjoyed the process of creating my business plan. It was like a game completing each section of the app that helped write a solid and professional business plan."
  - "I love it! This app makes it easier for me to make my business plan and think like an entrepreneur! Thank you, Centro!"
  - "This app is great! Easy to use, detailed, organized, and simple enough for anyone regardless of the level of experience." —Vernisha W.

Summary
We lead through our strong organizational values to guide our work to transform entrepreneurs to achieve their dreams. We value innovation, diversity, inclusion, freedom,

collaboration, and equity to help women and people of color from underserved communities thrive by realizing economic stability through entrepreneurship and asset-building to retire with dignity. We prove that the results of our efforts lead to greater social justice and racial equity.

Life is about following your dreams. Save your money and live within your means. Follow your heart. Lead with love and humility to help you realize your mission. Be courageous. Ask for help from others who are noble and willing to assist you in your mission. Ask for feedback from your peers and mentors. Make mistakes. It's okay to be wrong and embrace your failures because that is where the most significant lessons are learned. Little by little, you will see the fruits of your labor come alive and become the leader you were meant to be.

Key Lessons

1. *Embrace authenticity and be true to yourself; it is the foundation for genuine and meaningful impact.*
2. *Expand your horizons and venture beyond your immediate community by traveling and gaining a broader perspective. This exposure will provide valuable insights into the problem you aim to solve.*
3. *Challenge existing constructs, assumptions, and paradigms to push the boundaries and create innovative solutions beyond the status quo.*
4. *Break free from conventional thinking to design a better future.*
5. *Recognize that impact can manifest in various ways and forms. Take the time to observe and document the changes you witness, as this documentation will serve as a testament to the progress made and inspire further action.*

CHAPTER 9

LESSONS IN
LEADERSHIP AND
PERSONAL GROWTH

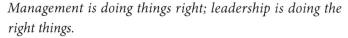

Management is doing things right; leadership is doing the right things.

—PETER F. DRUCKER

What does it take to be an effective nonprofit leader? How can someone prepare to lead a mission-focused and impactful community organization?

Becoming an effective nonprofit leader requires a multifaceted approach encompassing personal growth, continuous learning, and developing essential skills. Leaders can effectively navigate the complexities of leading mission-focused and impactful community organizations by cultivating empathy, logical thinking, effective communication, high standards, and balance. Embracing these qualities and experiences is essential for successful nonprofit leadership.

In this chapter, I delve into valuable lessons and experiences I've gained from the wisdom of others. Throughout my career, I recognized the importance of preparedness for leadership. To enhance my abilities, I actively sought guidance from esteemed leaders, teachers, and coaches willing to mentor me.

Personal Growth and Continuous Learning

A commitment to personal growth and continuous learning is crucial to excel as a nonprofit leader. This involves actively seeking opportunities for self-improvement, such as attending leadership workshops, pursuing advanced education, or participating in mentorship programs. By continually expanding one's knowledge and honing skills, leaders stay abreast of industry trends and best practices.

Cultivating Empathy

To serve a community effectively, you must feel genuine love and empathy for the people you aim to help. These emotions lie at the heart of effective leadership in the nonprofit sector. Understanding and relating to the experiences, challenges, and needs of the community being served is essential. By developing a deep sense of empathy, leaders foster meaningful connections, build trust, and develop impactful solutions in partnership with the community that addresses their most pressing issues. The willingness to support and witness their growth should stem naturally from your life experiences.

Embracing Logical Thinking

Nonprofit leaders must use analytical thinking and logic to drive decision-making and problem-solving. By developing skills in data analysis and critical thinking, leaders can make informed choices that maximize the impact of their organizations. This includes leveraging research, gathering relevant data, and applying logical frameworks to assess strategies and outcomes.

While studying at U.C. Berkeley, I worked as a research assistant to Professor Matthew Spiegel, a finance professor. He introduced me to the world of risk modeling. Professor Spiegel's mentorship helped me understand the importance of rigorous analysis and measuring data. It provided a solid foundation for building economic models and making informed decisions.

Effective Communication

Effective communication is a vital skill for any leader. Leaders should prioritize honing their verbal and written communication skills to articulate their vision, motivate their teams, and engage with stakeholders. By fostering transparent and open lines of communication, leaders can create a collaborative and inclusive environment that encourages innovation and progress.

Working under accomplished leaders taught me the power of clear and concise written communication. Developing strong writing skills enhances professional interactions and builds trust among team members. The ability to communicate ideas effectively helps convey a clear vision and expectations.

Upholding High Standards

Maintaining high standards is vital for nonprofit leaders to drive excellence and organizational growth and achieve impactful outcomes. By setting clear expectations, holding oneself and others accountable, and striving for continuous improvement, leaders can inspire their teams and create a culture of excellence. This commitment to high standards extends to all aspects of organizational operations, including program delivery, financial management, and ethical practices.

Through experiences in winemaking, I learned the importance of raising my standards in quality. Constructive feedback from a demanding mentor pushed me to improve and excel in my craft. Upholding high standards reflects personal integrity and commitment to excellence.

In my early twenties, I became passionate about winemaking when I visited Robert Mondavi Winery in Napa Valley for the first time during the harvest. I fell in love with the smells of freshly pressed grapes and the barrel room's fermentations. I could smell the yeast in the air and the wood from the fine French oak barrels. The experience made me happy, and I asked how to help and learn more. I would one day work as an intern at Ridge Vineyards on Montebello Ridge in the Santa Cruz Mountains.

Working in wineries is physically demanding. I sat before Paul Draper, asking to become an intern on his team. Paul was an icon and industry leader. He made wines that placed California on the world stage by beating the French wines in the famous Paris tasting competition in the 1970s. I got the internship, and Paul and his team taught me how to make fine wines. The work was physically challenging and exhausting.

I asked Paul for a final evaluation at the end of my internship. As I sat in his office, he looked stern, his hands on the desk and reading some papers. I was nervous about what he would say. He took his reading glasses off and looked me straight in the eye. He said, "Arturo, I'm disappointed in you." My throat formed a lump in it. "You were lazy, sloppy, and didn't work hard enough. You needed to learn to be more focused on the details. You have a gift for winemaking, so get serious!" He pounded his fist on the desk loudly.

I was traumatized by his brutal honesty, but Paul was right. I was late to work, on the phone with my girlfriend during working hours, or sometimes I did not pay attention to the detailed instructions I was provided. Furthermore, I didn't ask the questions I should have to gain a broader and deeper understanding of winemaking and vineyard management.

During my internship, Paul would welcome me every morning with seriousness. He would talk deeply about the natural winemaking process, the vineyard, and how to minimize manipulations of both. He focused on each detail, and the meticulous decisions started in the vineyard before the winemaking process commenced, resulting in high-quality, award-winning wines.

Inner Strength

Just as a fine wine exhibits balance and harmony, effective leadership requires balance in various aspects. Nonprofit leaders face numerous demands and challenges. Striking a balance between organizational goals, community needs, and available resources is essential. By managing time effectively, delegating tasks, and prioritizing strategically, leaders can optimize their efforts and ensure that limited resources are allocated efficiently. This balance extends to personal well-being, as leaders must prioritize self-care to sustain their energy and effectiveness.

My experience in martial arts taught me the importance of inner strength and harmony. Mastering self-defense techniques and training the mind and body helped me understand the interrelationship between mind, body, and spirit. Regular meditation and nurturing my inner chi contributed to a sense of peace and increased self-awareness.

I was taught this lesson again when I attended Golden Mountain Kung Fu, led by Master Sifu Valarie, in San Francisco. Master Sifu became my inspiration and mentor. Through her guidance, I learned self-defense and how to train my mind and body. Merriam-Webster's online dictionary defines "kung fu" as "any of various Chinese martial arts and related disciplines that are practiced especially for self-defense, exercise, and spiritual growth." For the first time in my life, I began to understand how to control my body, focus my concentration, and raise my awareness of my surroundings. She taught me to nurture my inner chi.

Regularly practicing kung fu resulted in endurance and inner strength. The lessons I learned deepened my respect for the interrelationship between my mind, body, and spirit.

Define Your Leadership Principles

Defining your leadership principles is an aspect of effective leadership. Through my personal experiences and the guidance of Frances Hesselbein, the former CEO of Girl Scouts of the USA and one of the most influential nonprofit leaders, I have gained valuable insights into the qualities and practices that shape impactful leadership in the nonprofit sector.

1. Craft Your Definition of Leadership: Frances encouraged me to create my definition of leadership, emphasizing that it extends beyond tasks and actions. Authentic leadership encompasses being honest and transparent. By reflecting on our values, purpose, and vision, we can shape a unique definition of leadership that aligns with our personal and organizational goals.
2. Focus on Being, Not Just Doing: Effective leadership is not solely about performing tasks; it involves embodying certain qualities and characteristics. Rather than fixating exclusively on what leaders should do, it is essential to cultivate who they should be. This includes fostering authenticity, integrity, empathy, and a growth mindset. By developing these attributes, leaders can inspire trust, build meaningful connections, and lead by example.
3. Character Determines Performance: The quality of character and consistency of a leader significantly impact the performance and results of the organization or mission they lead. Strong leadership qualities, such as integrity,

resilience, and a commitment to ethical practices, are vital for establishing a culture of excellence and driving positive outcomes. By embodying these qualities, leaders can foster a supportive and high-performing environment.

4. <u>Leadership Is Not Restricted to Position</u>: True leadership extends beyond formal organizational positions. It is a shared responsibility that can be demonstrated at all levels. Every individual has the potential to contribute as a leader, irrespective of their position. By recognizing and empowering others, leaders can harness their teams' collective talents and perspectives, fostering a culture of collaboration and innovation.

By embracing these principles, leaders in the nonprofit sector can inspire others, drive positive change, and create a thriving environment that contributes to the organization's mission and goals (Hesselbein 2002).

Influence through Humility

Humility plays a crucial role in effective nonprofit leadership. Humble leaders actively listen, admit mistakes and weaknesses, and prioritize the organization's greater good over personal recognition. By valuing the contributions of team members and creating an inclusive and appreciative environment, leaders can cultivate authenticity, build strong relationships, and inspire others to reach their full potential.

Living out your organization's stated values is essential to success as a leader. Consistency between words and actions establishes credibility and trust. By aligning your behavior with the organization's values, you set an example for others, fostering a culture of integrity and purpose.

Something to Be Sacrificed

Launching and growing a social venture or nonprofit organization often requires personal and professional sacrifices. Leaders must be prepared to invest significant time, effort, and financial resources into their mission. The willingness to sacrifice personal gain for the greater social impact demonstrates dedication and commitment to the cause. Financially, it often takes years for a nonprofit to compensate its staff.

These challenges may discourage many individuals from entering the field of social change-making. However, those driven by a sense of purpose and the desire to create a positive impact are willing to make these sacrifices, understanding that the fulfillment of their mission surpasses personal enrichment. My financial sacrifice would shock most people, but it would take ten years to receive the pay that enabled me to live comfortably. I was forty and entering the highest earning potential in my life when I started Centro Community Partners. But I would do it again. It was more important to me to serve my community.

Inner Knowing

Everyone possesses an inner knowing, which can be accessed through openness and receptiveness. This internal knowledge is often realized through a reflective state of mind, dreams, or intuition. It provides guidance and wisdom in overcoming challenges and navigating one's life. Cultivating the ability to tap into this inner knowing can be achieved through meditation, nature walks, silent prayer, or any activity that promotes stillness and silence in the mind. The power of inner knowing in decision-making is significant.

My inner knowing guided me into the unknown. It came through a series of dreams. After receiving trauma therapy, I dreamed of my mother, Olga. In the dream, tears were falling from her face. As I watched her, my tears fell. Then I saw a short, robust woman to my right open her arms and motion to me with her arms to come closer. I fell into her arms, and I woke up crying.

Days later, in another dream, the same woman who held me and spoke to me said, "I'm your grandmother. You must go to your ancestral lands." In awe, I was shocked since I did not know my grandmother. She died ten years before I was born. But I managed to respond and said, "I don't know where that is." She repeated, "You must go to your ancestral lands." I ignored what she told me as time passed and forgot about my dream. I dreamed a third time a month later, and my grandmother Julia returned. This time she said firmly, "You must return to your ancestral lands now!" Her voice was loud and impressed me with a sense of urgency. I needed to go. So, I purchased my ticket to Peru within two weeks to seek out my ancestral lands.

Lead by Faith

When it comes to leading by faith, this means embracing a leadership approach that is guided by trust, belief, and a higher purpose. One must be open to receiving guidance from a higher source or inner wisdom.

When I embarked on my journey to Peru, little did I know that it would lead me to discover my ancestral lands and fulfill a calling deeply rooted in faith. Following the advice of my uncle Juan, I traveled to Arequipa, where I had the extraordinary opportunity to connect with relatives I didn't know existed. The excitement of meeting these newfound family members was mutual, as they were eager to assist me in finding my grandmother's birthplace, the village of Ayo.

The road to Ayo was arduous as we traversed the hot desert, lush river valleys, and the majestic snowy Andes mountains on a narrow road that could barely accommodate two vehicles. The breathtaking views of desolate deserts, magnificent rivers, and snow-capped volcanoes gave us a vivid backdrop. As we ascended to the summit at eighteen thousand feet, I began to feel a peculiar sensation within me.

Just before midnight, as the bus reached the mountaintop, I sensed an unusual pressure on my chest, and tears welled in my eyes. Initially, I attributed these physical manifestations to the high altitude. However, as the situation unfolded, I became aware of its extraordinariness. I heard my grandmother, Julia, speaking to me with utmost clarity. Fully awake and receptive at that moment, I became a channel, bridging the gap between realms.

"My dear Arturo, I am overjoyed by your presence," my grandmother's voice resonated. "Now, I can again behold my cherished village through your eyes. I am Julia, and I long for the embrace of my home." During this otherworldly encounter, the boundaries between myself and my grandmother dissolved, and we became deeply connected. She conveyed her message, entrusting me with a significant task: to assist the community of Ayo and cultivate a vineyard—a calling deeply ingrained in our family heritage. I expressed my concerns about the environment and my lack of familiarity with the village, but her reassurance echoed in my ears, "Everything will be fine." Aware of the importance of preserving her identity, my grandmother conveyed messages to each of my siblings so they would recognize her presence. Diligently, I recorded her words on my smartphone, ensuring her message would not be lost. After engaging in this profound communion for approximately twenty to thirty minutes, I succumbed to exhaustion and drifted into a deep slumber.

When I awoke, I checked my phone and was astounded to find that I had captured our conversation—a testament to the reality of this extraordinary encounter. Our bus arrived in Ayo under darkness within two hours at 3:00 a.m. The village, nestled in the Valley of the Volcanoes, revealed itself as a humble abode of mud houses with scarce electricity. Illuminated by a mere streetlight, we navigated the dirt paths using headlamps until we reached the small house that would shelter us for the night.

The following day my cousin Rosario introduced me to my relatives. As I shared my lineage as Julia's grandchild, their disbelief mingled with delight. They were praying for someone with expertise in winemaking to come to Ayo and guide them. Astonishingly, I discovered that my great-grandfather and his brothers pioneered vineyard cultivation in Ayo during the early 1900s. Our family crafted wines for over a century, making Ayo a celebrated winemaking region. However, fewer family members chose to remain in the village with each generation, resulting in neglected vineyards and diminishing grape yields. My inner knowing affirmed that I was brought to Ayo from California, guided by my grandmother's plea for assistance. Embracing this responsibility, I embarked on a mission to revive the village's winemaking legacy.

Over the past three years, I have visited Ayo, each time bringing modern winemaking equipment and sharing contemporary viticulture practices. Through patient guidance, I have taught the villagers how to utilize the equipment, nurture their vineyards, and produce wines of exceptional quality and character. Collaborating with another family, a new vineyard is being established and employing modern techniques. We witnessed a remarkable transformation in 2020, 2021, and 2022 vintages as stable, delicious, commercial-grade wines replacing the previously vinegar-tainted wines.

The conviction of my inner voice and the unwavering faith that guided my path were justified—everything turned out fine. My reliance on faith, rather than mere visual confirmation, allowed me to embrace the journey, and in doing so, I fulfilled my mission.

Failure

Your experience helps to define the type of leader you will become. My personal and professional experiences taught me important lessons. I draw on these experiences when making leadership decisions. I was good at failing, and these failures taught me what I needed to know to start Centro. It helped me build a character of resilience and grit. I became open to failure since it happened so often in my work. As these failure experiences broke me down, I rebuilt myself to be more self-aware, empowered, and effective.

Summary

Becoming an effective nonprofit leader involves a combination of personal growth, continuous learning, and developing essential skills. Leaders can navigate the complexities of leading mission-focused and impactful community organizations through empathy, logical thinking, effective communication, high standards, and balance. Embracing these qualities and experiences can pave the way for successful nonprofit or social impact leadership.

Effective leadership involves embracing personal growth, continuous learning, and developing fundamental principles and qualities. Drawing inspiration from influential leaders like Frances Hesselbein, leaders can define leadership and focus on "how to be" rather than "how to do." Humility, sacrifice, and inner knowing are essential to successful social impact leadership. By embodying these principles, leaders can navigate challenges, build strong teams, and work on their organization's mission with dedication and purpose.

Learn to cultivate the skill of being still and quiet. It is a daily practice that will raise your self-awareness and ability to access the inner wisdom that helps to guide you through life. It's powerful. In practice, it may look like a meditative or dream state. Whether it manifests as your inner wisdom or inner voice, it contributes to your leadership and the "being" as a leader.

Key Lessons

- *Leadership inspires and guides others to a common goal while serving as a positive example.*
- *It is essential to remain humble and keep your ego in check, as authentic leadership is not about seeking personal recognition but uplifting and empowering others.*
- *Each individual should define their understanding of leadership based on their values, principles, and aspirations.*
- *Self-awareness is vital in leadership; knowing your character, strengths, and weaknesses allows you to leverage your strengths and work on areas of improvement.*
- *Cultivation through life experiences that challenge and transform you will help you grow and develop your leadership abilities.*
- *Effective leadership is recognized by its practical outcomes, such as fostering teamwork, driving innovation, and achieving tangible results.*
- *Fear is natural, but learning to overcome it, stepping outside your comfort zone, and embracing new growth opportunities is essential.*
- *Taking risks and relinquishing control is necessary to allow life to unfold and lead you to new destinations. Embracing curiosity and adopting a fresh perspective leads to transformative experiences.*
- *Being still and quiet allows you to listen to your inner voice, enabling deeper self-reflection, clarity of thought, and better decision-making.*

CHAPTER 10

TEAM BUILDING FOR SOCIAL IMPACT

The path to diversity begins with supporting, mentoring, and sponsoring diverse women and men to become leaders and entrepreneurs.

—DENISE MORRISON

Close your eyes for a moment and transport yourself back to the days when you picked teams on the playground. Remember the anticipation, the hopes of choosing the best players to form an unbeatable team? As we mature, the importance of team selection only grows, and our choices can shape our success and impact.

As you consider building an impact team, you must reflect on who will follow you and why they would choose to do so. When considering who will follow you and why, it's crucial to understand the team selection's impact on success or failure.

TEAM BUILDING FOR SOCIAL IMPACT · 153

So, make it easier on yourself, and take time to observe each individual before recruiting them to your team.

The skill of team building is often misunderstood or mishandled by many individuals. Common pitfalls include a lack of self-understanding, an inadequate understanding of organizational needs, or being driven by ego. These factors can lead to the formation of dysfunctional teams that are not optimized for creating social impact. The selection and recruitment process should be approached with care, thoughtfulness, and patience to build effective teams.

You will develop this skill over time as a leader, starting with a self-assessment. Before selecting volunteers or hiring staff, take the time to assess your abilities, weaknesses, and personal values. By understanding your strengths and weaknesses, you can identify the gaps that need to be filled with prospective teammates. For example, suppose you are a "big picture" type of person, like me, and have disadvantages like lack of attention to detail and conducting tedious tasks. In that case, it's important to recognize these areas and seek individuals who complement and excel in what you do not.

Bringing diverse perspectives and opportunities to the team can be a significant advantage when making decisions and working on your mission. Each team member's unique life experiences, shaped by their cultures and socioeconomic backgrounds, enrich the team. However, it's crucial to ensure everyone shares the same vision. Diversity creates opportunities for growth and learning. Fostering inclusivity and exploring different cultures helps us understand and embrace differences. By doing so, we can appreciate the unique contributions of each individual when they are included. You would encourage thoughtful commentary from staff even if they might not agree or that you value someone playing devil's advocate occasionally. You do not want staff that says "yes" whether they truly believe or not, but instead have risk-free, open communication, which allows everyone to be heard.

Assembling Your Team

When working for a cause that aims to bring about social change, it is important to carefully select team members who demonstrate dedication and commitment to the cause. Effective leadership involves making thoughtful decisions about who will join your team. This process takes time and requires a thorough examination of their character. To ensure the right fit, you can observe potential team members in their current roles or engage them in short-term projects as contractors or consultants before hiring. They must demonstrate character, values, work quality, work ethic, and strengths, as these factors contribute to their potential positive impact on the team and the community.

Sometimes, it is valuable to discover a "diamond in the rough." While it is unnecessary for potential team members to possess all the skills and abilities to fill every gap, they must exhibit the potential to learn and display a high-quality character. These recruits will need your guidance as they develop within the team, learning leadership lessons. Selecting the right team members is one aspect of leadership, but providing training and development is equally important. As a leader and change-maker, you must coach and train your teammates, preparing them well in transferrable skills so they can take on leadership roles themselves.

During my experience building the Centro team, I discovered that it is essential for each staff member to align with at least two personal values the organization shares. Why is this significant? Shared values form the foundation for an effective team to create organizational decisions. These values must be communicated from the beginning to ensure cohesion and alignment within the group; otherwise, conflicts may arise. By establishing shared values, you can ensure your team is on the same page and working together toward common goals.

First Staff Member

How can you attract a potential team member interested in conducting social impact and innovation? Naldo Peliks, when he expressed his desire to join Centro, initially offered his services as a volunteer. At the time, I needed assistance in supervising volunteer MBA student advisors. Naldo stood out due to his experience in technology consulting, and he had already completed his MBA. His unique strengths as an operations expert complemented my skills. One remarkable aspect of Naldo's problem-solving approach was his constant exploration of new processes and procedures, always looking at challenges through an innovative lens. As a result, Naldo assumed the role of Centro's chief operations officer and successfully established a robust system for program delivery, impact measurement, and technology development. Together, we formulated and implemented Centro's vision and strategic plans, and Naldo effectively operationalized them, ensuring the organization's success.

Diversity

Estefania Cardona, a former manager of programs and strategic relationships, offers valuable insight into her experience with Centro. When Estefania joined the organization, she noticed a strong alignment between her values and the organization's mission. She was attracted to Centro because it stood out from the typical nonprofit stereotype of disorganization and burnout. Instead, she wanted to be part of a sustainable organization that aimed to impact the community positively.

Working in a culturally and socially diverse environment was another significant motivator for Estefania. She emphasized the importance of embracing diversity by bringing together people from different backgrounds and allowing them to contribute their unique perspectives and ways of doing things. Estefania believed the team could achieve the same goal using different approaches by listening, changing, adapting, and harnessing the best from everyone. This diversity of perspectives fosters greater productivity, creativity, and impact.

Estefania's project approach balanced discipline and structure with a strong belief in doing things right. She valued caring and pushed herself and her team members to improve performance. Her attributes brought value to the Centro team and contributed to the organization's culture. Estefania faced challenges as an immigrant woman of color, but

Centro allowed her to break through paradigms and make a meaningful difference. She appreciated Centro's room to grow and deeply cared for the organization.

In 2015, I worked with Estefania while piloting an entrepreneurship boot camp program in Medellin, Colombia. We met through a mutual friend when I asked if I could teach a social entrepreneurship course at her coworking space. Estefania joined my class and helped me to recruit entrepreneurs for the course, allowing me to get to know her and her perspective on social mission organizations. I recognized her leadership qualities, so I invited Estefania to join the Centro team in the United States. She came to Oakland, California, and played a key role in facilitating Centro's basic entrepreneurship programs in Spanish, contributing to developing procedures and processes for the programs team.

Staff Appreciation

Building a culture of appreciation within your team is crucial for fostering a sense of value and belonging. Estefania Cardona played a significant role in introducing the importance of staff appreciation at Centro. Initially, our team didn't prioritize celebrating wins or acknowledging setbacks, as we were focused on overcoming challenges and moving forward. However, as our team expanded, it became evident that it was essential to appreciate team members' contributions. Estefania recognized the power of appreciation, stating that it allows individuals to be seen and heard.

At Centro, our staff consists mainly of immigrants or the children of immigrants, contributing to a global growth mindset and a cohesive, inclusive environment. Despite working in different countries, we celebrate our team members' diverse backgrounds and successes and even enjoy sharing different cuisines from various cultures. Our culture of appreciation ensures everyone feels valued, regardless of their location. These organizational practices contribute to the diversity and growth of our team.

Community Is Reflected in the Team

Estefania emphasizes the significance of acknowledging her identity as an immigrant woman of color: "Being recognized in this capacity is important to me because I represent the very community that Centro serves." Her perspective highlights a fundamental principle in building a team that aligns with the community we aim to support. By including individuals from diverse backgrounds, including immigrants, low-income women, and people of color, we gain invaluable insights that enable us to develop curricula and programs that genuinely address the community's needs. Estefania's contribution to the team ensured our programs were relevant, inclusive, and impactful.

Freedom to Create Your Role

Verónica Gutiérrez, the former capital access manager at Centro, brings a unique perspective on her decision to join our organization. As an immigrant from Chile, Verónica's previous experience was working at Kiva International, with whom we established a partnership to provide no-interest microloans for capital access. Verónica was highly recommended for her role at Centro, and she shares her reasons for choosing to work with us: "I believe the work environment plays an important role in shaping your experience and developing your skills. In my past jobs, I sought a safe environment that would enable me to learn and prepare myself professionally for new tasks, activities, and projects. However, finding a healthy work environment can be challenging. Sometimes you don't have the best manager or colleagues, and the projects may not align with your aspirations."

She highlights the importance of actively involving team members in defining their roles and strategies, empowering them to take ownership of their positions. Reflecting on her experience, she recalls, "When I joined Centro, I was assigned to a new position leading the access to capital. I was free to shape and create aspects of my role that would best position me for learning, growth, and innovation. This freedom was the catalyst for bringing something new and innovative to life." She adds, "My manager encouraged me to explore the opportunities within the new role, become an expert, and prepare myself to achieve our shared goals." Verónica believes this approach is essential for building a high-performing team dedicated to making a social impact.

Verónica also shares a contrasting story from her experience in Chile, where proposing new ideas in a new role led to conflict and resistance from her team members. They questioned her ability to contribute as a newcomer. This challenging situation created hesitations and demoralization for Verónica, making navigating her ideas and projects difficult. In stark contrast, Verónica emphasizes the supportive environment at Centro, saying, "At Centro, it's different. They are open and encouraging if you have a new idea and want to present it to your teammates. I hadn't experienced rejection or negative responses. It's a key feature of an innovative environment that fosters openness to new ideas and growth." As a result, Verónica learns from her colleagues' reactions and feedback, continuously improving her new ideas to benefit the team and Centro. For both Estefania and Verónica, Centro was a stepping stone to greater leadership positions that awaited them. We are grateful for their impactful contributions at Centro.

Developing Volunteers to Lead

Development and fundraising are key functions at Centro, and Damanbir Singh, the development manager, plays a key role in leading grant development and fundraising efforts. Originally from India, Damanbir's journey with Centro began in 2012 when he joined as a volunteer MBA student advisor, coaching and mentoring entrepreneurs. Eventually, he transitioned into his current position overseeing grant development.

Reflecting on his initial acceptance of the grant development role, Damanbir shares, "When I was offered the opportunity to take on the grant writing role, I wasn't sure it would work out, to be honest. I even asked Arturo if he was sure about choosing me for this position. However, I accepted the offer because I didn't have another job lined up. I wasn't fully aware of what I got myself into. That was back in 2016, and now, fast forward to today in 2023; my love for the work we do in the community keeps bringing me back. It's gratifying to know that the funds I help raise support a noble cause, such as providing entrepreneurship education and access to capital for low-income women and minorities. This knowledge gives me the courage to approach funders and donors, knowing their contributions will positively impact people's lives."

Damanbir also emphasizes the importance of the Centro team in his experience. He admires how the team functions seamlessly, likening it to a well-oiled machine. Each member possesses deep knowledge in their respective areas: programs, finance, or operations. The systems and infrastructure developed over the past two years have contributed to making more informed decisions and setting achievable goals. Furthermore, Damanbir appreciates the personal care and support he receives from his teammates, both professionally and emotionally. This aspect of a supportive work environment is crucial and contributes to his overall happiness and satisfaction in doing his work at Centro.

Drucker on Roles & Responsibilities

When building the team at Centro, I implemented two crucial teachings to ensure we hired the most suitable individuals for each position. The first lesson, inspired by Peter F. Drucker's book *Management: Tasks, Responsibilities, Practices*, emphasized the importance of thoroughly evaluating prospective team members for their compatibility with the role. This evaluation process involved assessing how their abilities, skills, and talents aligned with the responsibilities and deliverables of the position. Taking the time to observe and search for indications that the new hire would thrive and find fulfillment in the role in the long run, was essential. This deliberate approach ensured we selected individuals who had the potential to grow and contribute to Centro for years to come (Drucker 1973).

The second fundamental principle I learned in recruiting was identifying a candidate's adaptability and independence. I sought to determine how well they could perform without detailed information, formal structures, and constant supervision. Could they proactively seek out their sources of information, establish their work processes and structure, and effectively manage themselves to deliver high-quality work? These qualities of adaptability and self-sufficiency were highly valued in potential recruits for Centro's team. We sought individuals who could navigate ambiguous situations, take the initiative, and exhibit self-discipline to achieve excellent results.

By integrating these teachings into our recruitment process, we prioritize finding the best individuals for each role within Centro's team. We understand the importance of selecting candidates with the necessary skills and capabilities and the potential to grow and assume leadership positions within the organization.

Why Nonprofits Experience High Turnover

How to avoid the pitfalls that lead to employee turnover? According to the Nonprofit Employment Practices Survey and *Chronicle of Philanthropy*, the staff turnover rate for the nonprofit industry is 19 percent compared to 17.8 percent for all other industries (IPM Advancement 2023). The nonprofit sector is the third largest employer, representing about 10 percent of the US workforce. The top reasons people leave nonprofits are burnout, lack of benefits, excessive workloads, no career advancement, no professional development, and toxic workplace cultures (Salamon and Newhouse 2020).

According to a labor report from the US Bureau of Labor Statistics in 2020, employees typically work for their current employer for an average of four years. At Centro, we place great importance on individuals' decisions because our work is challenging. We also recognize there comes a time when employees may need to move on in their careers, whether due to a better fit elsewhere or the evolving nature of their roles, as our organization grows and requires new skill sets. These conversations surrounding staff transitioning to different positions or even parting with the organization are difficult but necessary. However, they are an integral part of organizational development and change. Our goal is to build the best possible team for the period of growth ahead, allowing existing staff members to adapt to upcoming changes or explore new leadership opportunities outside of Centro.

Summary

Effective team building requires self-assessment, organizational needs, and a commitment to filling gaps with diverse teammates. Embracing diversity and inclusivity provides an opportunity to leverage different perspectives, creating a more well-rounded and successful team. By maintaining a shared vision, we can harness the power of diversity to achieve our collective goals and a more significant impact.

I hope other nonprofits that look to thrive can see the value of developing a diverse team, a culture of appreciation, and an innovative environment. Recruiting should be a patient management practice requiring observing people who can grow with the role and expand it as needed to reach greater performance levels. Cultivating and coaching the team into leaders ensures a solid foundation of professional skills and abilities that are imparted, shared, and celebrated.

Key Lessons

- *Foster a culture of inclusivity and foster a sense of belonging within your team, acknowledging and celebrating achievements.*
- *When building a team, actively seek out diversity and encourage team members to bring their unique perspectives and approaches to problem-solving.*
- *Prioritize alignment of core values when considering potential recruits, ensuring their beliefs and principles align with the organization's shared values.*
- *Recognize the importance of representation by building a team that reflects the diverse backgrounds and experiences of the communities and individuals your organization serves.*
- *Take the time to understand your organization's specific needs and define roles and responsibilities that align with those needs, seeking team members who can provide long-term value and contribute to the organization's success.*

CHAPTER 11

WISDOM FROM THE TEAM: LESSONS LEARNED

Ultimately, there is no such thing as failure. There are lessons learned in different ways.

—TWYLA THARP

In the fast-paced and dynamic landscape of nonprofit and social enterprise leadership, one thing remains constant: the imperative of investing in innovation, technology, talent, and professional development. These pillars are the foundation for organizations to survive, evolve, and thrive in their mission to create lasting impact and sustainability. Neglecting these critical areas is akin to setting oneself up for failure and an inability to endure the challenges in our work environment.

Before establishing a nonprofit or social enterprise, seeking advice and insight from experienced social impact leaders becomes invaluable. By learning from their accumulated wisdom, one gains a valuable advantage—a sneak preview of potential pitfalls to avoid and a better understanding of what lies ahead. I encountered hurdles when I sought guidance from established nonprofit leaders in my industry. Many nonprofit leaders didn't meet me when I established Centro because they were too busy. However, this experience fueled my determination to share my knowledge and experiences with anyone willing to listen. I firmly believe in encouraging collaboration among impact leaders to create a more positive global impact.

Also, keeping volunteers engaged and accountable was a challenge, but we did manage to understand the motivation of volunteers, such as being challenged and learning transferrable skills. In the best cases, our volunteers would become Centro employees.

The disparity between successful nonprofits and those that falter is evident in sobering statistics. A staggering 30 percent of nonprofits fail to operate after a decade, and over half of the registered nonprofits in the US operate with less than thirty days of cash reserves (NCCS 2020). Understanding the reasons why nonprofits fail is crucial. Poor leadership, inadequate planning, unrealistic expectations, financial constraints, a failure to adapt, and insufficient technology are common culprits of nonprofit failures (McRae 2022). To ensure triumph, it is imperative to steer clear of these known pitfalls.

With the spirit of sharing knowledge and fostering growth, the Centro team offers helpful tips and lessons learned since our inception in 2010. We strive to guide future social impact leaders and practitioners through essential areas such as operations and technology, curriculum development and training, programs, strategic partnerships, and access to capital. By sharing these valuable insights, we aspire to contribute to the success of others and ignite a collective force for positive change in the world.

Operations & Technology

Naldo Peliks, our esteemed chief operations officer, offers his insightful perspective on the vital role of innovation and key considerations for developing technology within your nonprofit or social enterprise to drive impact and scale. With his expertise, Naldo played a pivotal role in developing the Centro app and spearheaded the creation of our technology platforms, enabling us to effectively deliver our programs to our communities.

- **Unlocking the Value of Technology:** Our firsthand experience revealed the transformative power of technology in driving efficiency and scalability. Through rigorous testing of our Centro app prototype, we witnessed significant cost savings in our programs while achieving comparable outcomes. Leveraging technology is instrumental in creating a scalable, cost-effective avenue to support those in need.
- **Embracing Technological Limitations:** It is crucial to acknowledge the boundaries of technology and design solutions that account for these limitations. By employing the Centro app to gather essential information from entrepreneurs before workshops, we optimize their

workshop experience and provide tailored support that caters to their specific needs.

- **Breaking Projects into Manageable Pieces:** When presenting our inspiring roadmap, we encountered enthusiasm from funders and developers who wished to tackle everything simultaneously. However, breaking the project into smaller components and adopting project scrum methodology helped us achieve incremental progress and continually enhance our support for entrepreneurs. This approach facilitates effective collaboration among teams working on complex products.

- **Investing in Skilled Developers:** Overcoming the challenge of keeping volunteer developers accountable proved demanding, especially when competing with their other commitments. By outsourcing development tasks and sharing project management responsibilities, we have significantly improved our ability to complete projects successfully and adhere to established timelines. This strategic move recognizes the Centro app's and other technological platforms' central role in our model as we expand our infrastructure.

- **Embracing Change:** Technology is in a constant state of evolution. While our decisions today influence our future options, it is vital to anticipate ongoing adjustments over time. We must remain adaptable and responsive to emerging technological advancements.

- **Seeking Expert Guidance:** As technology evolves and options multiply, seeking expert advice becomes indispensable in our decision-making process. Currently, we benefit from the expertise of outsourced Centro app developers and strategic technology advisors who offer valuable insights for our technological endeavors.

- **Embracing Minimum Viable Products (MVPs):** Our approach has evolved through an iterative process that emphasizes the creation of MVPs. Before the Centro app's inception, our curriculum and methods underwent multiple iterations, refining them through trainer-led workshops and direct interactions with entrepreneurs. Practicing quick, simple, and cost-effective ways to test our methodologies, we have streamlined the development process, guided by invaluable feedback from our entrepreneurs.
- **Understanding Our Identity:** While technology is pivotal in Centro's delivery model, we must remember we are not a technology firm. We leverage technology to enhance our impact and support, but our core focus remains on our mission and the communities we serve.
- **Incorporating Time Buffers:** We based our timelines on the developer's early feedback and always got it wrong. Recognizing the uncertainties of development timelines, we have learned to incorporate buffers by doubling the estimates provided by developers. This approach minimizes the risks associated with potential delays, ensuring our projects stay on track and sometimes ahead of schedule.
- **Worry Less about the Edge Cases**: Avoid edge cases (that don't impact most people), taking the focus away from priorities. By assigning priorities to issues, we can weed out the edge cases and focus on features and improvements that help most of the people we serve. Similarly, we've learned to focus on what happens versus overthinking scenarios that might occur.
- **Prioritizing Core Focus:** Avoiding distractions from edge cases with limited impact on the majority is crucial.

Assign clear priorities to issues. We prioritized features and improvements that benefit most individuals we serve rather than overextending resources on less common scenarios. Similarly, we've learned to focus on what happens versus overthinking scenarios that might occur.

Entrepreneurship Curriculum Development & Training

DJ Healy's tenure at Centro spanned over a decade, during which he made significant contributions to our organization. Starting as an MBA volunteer advisor to entrepreneurs, he gradually became a senior entrepreneur trainer and played a pivotal role in developing our renowned Centro app and curriculum. Today, he imparts invaluable insights derived from his extensive experience.

While some of these lessons may appear cliché, their underlying wisdom becomes evident upon deep reflection. They remind us of the continuous growth we can achieve and the areas we can strive for improvement. As I review these lessons, I recognize they encompass the lessons I have learned and the areas in which I can further excel, highlighting the importance of ongoing self-improvement.

- **Release Your Ego:** Above all else, this lesson stands at the core. It entails actively listening rather than telling, embracing failure, self-critiquing before seeking external criticism, practicing humility, and graciously accepting praise. The journey begins by letting go of your ego and recognizing that the moment you believe you have it all figured out is the moment you've already lost.

- **Embrace Surrender:** Instead of trying to mold the world according to your plans, learn to immerse yourself in the community you aim to serve. You can move forward more resiliently by attentively observing and adapting to the circumstances. Remember, one could have a well-thought-out plan until unexpected challenges arise, so be ready to relinquish rigid plans when necessary.
- **Cultivate Silence and Listening:** As Stephen Covey aptly stated, "Seek first to understand before seeking to be understood." The significance of this practice cannot be overstated, nor can its difficulty be undermined. Mastering the art of attentive listening is vital.
- **Get Buy-In:** To motivate and engage others effectively, make them feel heard and valued by actively listening and involving them in decision-making. Genuine buy-in comes from creating an environment of inclusivity and collaboration.
- **Be Honest and Courageous:** Being honest, whether with oneself or others, demands immense courage. It means standing up for your beliefs, expressing unpopular opinions, or risking potential offense. Please do not shy away from temporary conflict when it paves the way for long-term benefits. This is the difference between being polite and nice on the one hand and being kind on the other (not to say you shouldn't be polite and nice, just not at the expense of being honest).
- **Be Yourself:** Building upon the previous point, learning to be comfortable in your skin is crucial for honesty and cultivating the courage to express yourself genuinely. This authenticity is vital for sustainability and personal satisfaction in your work.

- **Simplify and Seek Elegance:** Strive for simplicity and elegance in all endeavors. It's a lesson that I, too, struggle with and consistently learn the hard way. Instead of rigid rules, embrace simple, practical methods and trial-and-error approaches when developing processes. Ask questions precisely and explore evidence thoroughly.
- **Understand Trade-Offs:** One of the most valuable questions I've learned at Centro is, "If we are going to say yes to this, what are we saying no to?" The most crucial point about this question recognizes that every time you say yes to something, you are always saying no to something else. (Hint: If you think you don't know what you're saying no to, you're probably saying no to doing a good job of it.)
- **Foster Precision:** Communication often opens doors to misinterpretation. Generalizations, attributions, intonations, and body language all present opportunities for misunderstanding. When conveying important information, strive to be precise in your language.
- **Sympathy, Compassion, and Empathy:** Sympathy involves feeling sorry for someone, compassion entails caring about them, and empathy centers around understanding them. When empathy is present, sympathy and compassion naturally follow, although the reverse is not always true. However, being sympathetic and compassionate doesn't guarantee empathy.

Programs & Strategic Partnerships

Estefania Cardona, our former programs and strategic partnership manager, brings invaluable insights and lessons from her experience overseeing our program operations and collaborating with community partners. Under her leadership, our organization witnessed significant growth, expanding our reach from serving approximately 150 entrepreneurs to over 500 annually. Estefania and her team have played a vital role in developing the systems that enabled us to create and scale our programs effectively across California and New York.

- **Learn, Test, Evaluate, Improve & Repeat:** Centro embraces this methodology for project development, emphasizing the importance of piloting ideas and swiftly adapting to environmental changes.
- **Effective Feedback and Clear Expectations:** Establishing feedback loops and fostering clear communication channels with stakeholders is important for internal and external relationships.
- **Infrastructure Shapes Behavior:** Building a sustainable program requires a well-designed infrastructure that streamlines processes, eliminates manual work, and allows for strategic thinking.
- **Lead by Example:** Our commitment to training extends not only to entrepreneurs but also to our trainers. The curriculum is thoroughly tested to ensure its cultural relevance and impact.
- **Frameworks for Efficiency:** Creating frameworks for communication, process documentation, project development, and delegation enhances teamwork and efficiency.
- **Research and Resourcefulness:** Cultivate curiosity, problem-solving, asking questions, and resourcefulness. This enables us to work with diverse resources, bridge accessibility gaps, and better serve entrepreneurs.

- **Nurture Partnerships:** Community-based organizations that share our mission can be valuable partners. Embrace collaboration and foster mutually beneficial relationships.
- **Strengthen Your Core Competence:** Focus on what you do best and continuously excel at it. Centro's core competence lies in creating and delivering effective and impactful training programs for entrepreneurs and trainers.
- **Celebrate Diversity:** Recognize and appreciate the unique strengths, perspectives, and working styles that diversity brings to the team.
- **Navigate Change:** Embrace the world's constant evolution and develop a mindset open to change. Adapting and maintaining integrity as individuals and organizations are key to success.

Access to Capital

Verónica Gutiérrez was pivotal in establishing and spearheading the Centro Capital Access Hub, an initiative to assist entrepreneurs in accessing microloans and grants. Her primary focus revolved around equipping entrepreneurs with the necessary skills and knowledge to apply for and secure capital to launch and expand their businesses. While Centro is not a direct provider of capital, it functions as a vital hub within the community, collaborating with a network of loan providers and offering the necessary funding. Verónica's invaluable experience and expertise have been instrumental in building our robust "access to capital" program, which facilitates allocating millions of dollars in capital for new and emerging businesses within the community.

- **Patience in Acquiring Funding:** It is essential to acknowledge that securing funding is a process that requires time. As advisors, we assist entrepreneurs in developing a well-structured plan, organizing their business information, and establishing realistic expectations for the lending or grant application process.
- **Developing a Funding Strategy:** A successful experience with loans or grants necessitates the creation of a comprehensive strategy. We guide entrepreneurs in crafting a plan that considers various scenarios and sets goals, considering the potential challenges they may encounter.
- **Program Graduation Does Not Equate to Loan Readiness:** Recognizing that entrepreneurs enter our programs at different stages of their planning process, we support them in becoming loan-ready. We assist in formulating business plans, facilitating decision-making, and assigning tasks that contribute to their overall preparedness.
- **Sustaining Communication:** Maintaining consistent communication with entrepreneurs is crucial for a successful repayment experience of the microloan. Following the loan disbursement, we stay in touch, provide updates, and monitor their business's progress. Regular communication enables us to identify and address potential issues promptly.
- **Establishing Strategic Partnerships:** Nurturing ongoing coordination and collaboration with local lenders and organizations enhances the success of the Centro Capital Access Hub dramatically. This facilitates the sharing of up-to-date resources and timely information within our community.
- **Dedication of Time by Entrepreneurs:** Applying for loans and grants requires a similar amount of time and

effort. It is a misconception to perceive grants as more accessible because they are often considered "free money." Both funding opportunities necessitate thorough preparation, including documentation, business planning, and clearly articulating the value proposition.

- **Time Investment for Loan Readiness:** As we guide entrepreneurs through the loan application, managing expectations and evaluating their financial readiness is important. This involves identifying suitable lenders, assessing their likelihood of qualification, and mitigating potential risks such as nonpayment or bankruptcy.
- **Comprehensive Support Assessment:** To ensure a successful capital acquisition experience, we combine our assistance in loan applications with one-on-one support to define the next steps for the business. In collaboration with trainers, this holistic approach helps entrepreneurs identify additional requirements.
- **Anticipating Market Changes:** We maintain an organic and proactive connection with the entrepreneurial ecosystem to stay abreast of market changes and identify new opportunities. This allows us to adapt our services, consider new loan products or grants, and better support our entrepreneurs' needs.

The Centro team offers some powerful lessons, thoughts, and insights. We are a small but mighty team. We are decisive and effective in our approach. We love our work as we execute, innovate, create, and impact the communities we serve daily. These insights came as a result of overcoming the challenges that keep most nonprofits or social enterprises from succeeding. We don't forget why most nonprofits fail to stay open within the first years and why 30 percent fail after ten years (Morris, Wyman, Roberts, et al. 2018).

Summary

We are grateful to the Centro team for generously sharing their lessons and insights, which can guide you in your decision-making process. By following these insights and lessons learned, we have navigated the complexities of technology implementation while staying true to our mission of creating lasting impact and meaningful change in the lives of those we serve. We eagerly welcome collaborations with the community and are delighted to continue sharing more about our approach at Centro.

Your endeavors in establishing and growing your nonprofit or social enterprise will be a transformative journey. Begin by formulating a well-thought-out plan, actively listening to the individuals you aim to assist or the cause you wish to champion, and maintaining adaptability to navigate the fluid currents. Regardless of your age, this pursuit will become one of your most extraordinary endeavors as you engage in the business of transformation.

CHAPTER 12

A COMPLETE ECONOMIC DEVELOPMENT SYSTEM

There is no law against living below your means and then saving and investing what is left.

—MOKOKOMA MOKHONOANA.

Are you prepared for your retirement years? Whether or not you're a social impact entrepreneur, planning and saving for retirement is crucial. At Centro, we've noticed a growing concern among our successful program graduates who return to us seeking guidance on retirement savings. Today, we want to emphasize the importance of cultivating savings and investment habits among entrepreneurs once they've achieved stability in their businesses.

Centro recognizes we've only addressed the initial phase of the economic development system that leads to wealth generation. We understand entrepreneurs typically experience the challenges of starting and growing their businesses for the first two to three years. However, once they reach this point, their businesses begin to generate profits and provide a stable source of income. The next critical step is for entrepreneurs to allocate a percentage of their earnings for retirement savings over the next ten to twenty years. Unfortunately, during this phase, we have yet to establish a comprehensive component within the economic development system focusing on asset-building and wealth creation. This chapter will delve into the current state of savings and investments and shed light on the disparities for low-income individuals, particularly people of color.

Asset-Building Leads to Economic Prosperity

Why aren't more people prioritizing savings? For the past two decades, the savings rates in the United States have fluctuated between 3 percent and 7 percent of disposable income (US Bureau of Economic Analysis 2023). At Centro, we closely examine how entrepreneurs from our programs generate income and contribute to job creation within their communities once their businesses are established. As we explore the potential for these businesses to build assets, we aim to foster a cycle of long-term economic prosperity.

Starting small businesses can indeed provide entrepreneurs with a stable source of income. However, amidst their focus on reinvesting in business growth, we wonder: Are these entrepreneurs also saving for emergencies or retirement?

While Centro successfully developed its robust programs to assist low-income entrepreneurs in launching and expanding their small businesses, we recognize the next phase of our evolution lies in completing the economic development system through asset-building. By embracing asset-building, entrepreneurs of color can achieve more than financial stability and unlock opportunities for economic mobility, transitioning from low-to-moderate-to-middle-income brackets and ultimately breaking free from the constraints of poverty.

The vision at Centro encompasses the development of an economic development system that contains asset-building. This will be part of our evolution and a new program component. We aspire to see the program's graduates create generational wealth that uplifts their lives and strengthens their communities. Let us explore the significance of asset-building and its transformative potential in fostering long-term prosperity.

Learning from the Master

From a young age, my mother instilled in me the value of saving. I vividly remember the day she took me to the local Barclays Bank in Santa Clara, California, at eleven years old to open my first savings account. She had a unique approach to teaching me about money. She said, "I want you to learn how to save money, so when you deposit money, I will match it." At first, I was puzzled because I had no money. But my mother had a plan. She encouraged me to help our neighbors by offering services like washing cars and cutting lawns. I had yet to learn that people would pay for such work. But with my mom's guidance and motivation, I began taking on odd jobs around the neighborhood, just as she envisioned.

She encouraged me to deposit my earnings in our neighborhood bank, and she would match my savings. My mother was an exceptional teacher when it came to money.

Throughout my upbringing, I drew inspiration from my immigrant mother, Olga. In Lima, Peru, during challenging times of high unemployment and civil unrest in the early 1960s, she single-handedly supported our family through her entrepreneurial endeavors. Olga sold dolls and prepared food for construction workers to provide for my five older siblings. She was part of a remarkable generation of resilient, talented, creative, and resourceful women born amid the Great Depression in the 1930s. Circumstances forced her into entrepreneurship, and she embraced it wholeheartedly.

In the early 1960s, my father, Oscar, immigrated to the United States for work in Colorado. This left Olga alone to care for my five siblings in Peru, ages three months to ten years old. Financial support from my father was not feasible during his initial years in a new country, working as a carpenter alongside his brothers. Consequently, my mother found ways to make ends meet. These were tough times for her.

Fortunately, Olga possessed honed sewing skills and was a talented seamstress. Her idea was to sell dolls, but she needed some startup capital. Since formal credit or microloan options were unavailable, she convinced our uncle Tito to help her. Recognizing her natural business acumen, Tito agreed to partner with her. He owned a small, manufactured factory of plastic toys, making him the perfect collaborator for Olga's venture.

Determined and resourceful, Olga approached her cousins, also skilled seamstresses, and requested fabric scraps from them. With these scraps, she diligently crafted unique and colorful dresses for her dolls, paying careful attention to every detail. She displayed the dolls beautifully in cardboard boxes, laid out on tablecloths, and caught the buyer's attention. Her high-quality dolls quickly sold out, and her sales began to grow. This success brought immense joy to Olga, affirming her belief that she could make things happen through planning, risk-taking, and unwavering confidence in her abilities.

Before long, Olga repaid our uncle Tito for the dolls and accumulated enough savings to support our family through the challenging times. Her resilience and hard work paid off, and she taught me invaluable lessons about determination, faith, and the power of saving.

Reflecting on those early experiences and the entrepreneurial spirit of my mother, I am reminded of the importance of financial independence and its impact on individuals and families. Saving money is a means to overcome immediate hardships and a pathway to long-term stability and prosperity. My mother's teachings continue to guide me as I strive to help others on their journey to financial security and success.

US Savings & Investing Habits

Savings and investing habits in the United States vary significantly across different racial and ethnic groups. While only some learn about saving money from their parents, it is worth noting that people of color face unique challenges when building wealth. Statistics reveal that people of color are less likely to have savings accounts than White Americans (Caporal and Daly 2023). However, they tend to save more on average when they have savings accounts. According to the Federal Reserve, only 44 percent of Black Americans have a retirement savings account with a balance of around $20,000, while 65 percent of White Americans have an average balance of $50,000. These disparities also extend to equity investments, where only 34 percent of Black American households own such assets, in contrast to 61 percent of White families. Moreover, the average value of stocks owned by Black Americans is significantly lower, amounting to only $14,400, roughly a quarter of what their White counterparts hold.

When examining gender disparities, it becomes apparent that a considerable percentage of Black women are not invested in anything, with 59 percent lacking any investments. Comparatively, 48 percent of Hispanic women, 34 percent of White women, and 23 percent of White men are not invested (Bhutta et al. 2019). These numbers highlight the financial gaps and challenges faced by different demographic groups in the United States.

These disparities in savings and investments have significant implications for net worth. Approximately one-third of people of color have appreciable assets such as stocks, mutual funds, bonds, and exchange-traded funds, in contrast to 60 percent of White households. With fewer people of color holding assets, the majority miss out on the benefits of compound interest, which, over time, can provide higher average returns and contribute to wealth accumulation.

These findings highlight the urgent need to address the systemic barriers and inequalities preventing equal financial opportunities for marginalized communities. By addressing these disparities and promoting financial literacy and inclusion, we can strive for a more equitable society where we create the opportunity to build wealth and secure our community's financial future.

The following table shows the difference in asset type by race.

Asset Type	White	Black	Hispanic	Other
Primary Residence	73%	45%	46%	54%
Vehicle	90%	73%	80%	80%
Retirement Accounts	60%	34%	30%	48%
Family-owned Business Equity	15%	7%	6%	13%
Stocks	61%	31%	28%	47%

Source: 2019 US Federal Reserve's Triennial Survey of Consumer Finances (Bhutta et al. 2019)

A significant disparity exists between people of color and White households regarding home ownership. Less than half of people of color possess a primary residence as an asset, whereas more than 70 percent of White households own their homes. Analyzing the composition of net worth within the US middle class, we find that approximately 80 percent is derived from home ownership (61.9 percent) and retirement funds (16.6 percent). Other liquid assets, such as cash savings, contribute 8.5 percent, while income from stocks and bonds accounts for 3.9 percent. Regarding business ownership is 7.9 percent, and miscellaneous assets constitute 1.2 percent (Routley 2019).

The wealth disparities among families of different racial groups, as highlighted in a 2019 Survey of Consumer Finances report, are striking. White families possess eight times the median wealth compared to Black families, with a median wealth of $188,200 for Whites and only $24,100 for Blacks. Similarly, White families have five times the median wealth of Hispanic families, with a median wealth of $36,050 for Hispanics (Bhutta et al. 2019).

The racial wealth gap in the United States is evident when examining net worth breakdown by race. The table demonstrates the significant disparities between White and people of color, specifically Black and Hispanics/Latinos. These disparities can primarily be attributed to systemic disadvantages that create obstacles to asset accumulation and wealth generation within these groups.

Race	Median Net Worth in 2019
Black	$24,100
Hispanics/Latinx	$36,050
White	$188,200

Source: 2019 Survey of Consumer Finances

Financial Nightmare

In my household, my parents approached managing money differently. While my mother was a saver, my father was a spender who relied heavily on credit cards. Unfortunately, his spending habits led him into debt. Witnessing these contrasting behaviors, I learned the importance of saving money and opened my savings account early in life. However, once I entered college, I started using credit cards readily available on campus. I quickly fell into the trap of accumulating debt, primarily due to high-interest rates and excessive use.

I was ashamed and realized I lacked the self-control to handle credit cards responsibly. The speed at which the interest on my balances grew was alarming, causing my debt to spiral out of control. Struggling to make monthly payments, I began receiving relentless calls from collection agencies, which was a demoralizing and traumatic experience. Recognizing that I needed assistance, I contacted a San Francisco nonprofit called Credit Counselors for guidance in resolving my financial despair.

With their help, I enrolled in a five-year repayment plan. As part of the process, I closed all my credit card accounts and learned to budget my expenses using only cash. Determined to regain control of my financial situation, I diligently stuck to the payment plan and eventually freed myself from credit card debt. This experience taught me the corrosive nature of credit card debt and the importance of avoiding it. On the other hand, certain debts like mortgages, depending on the housing market and economy, can be considered healthy as they have the potential to build equity and net worth, unlike credit card debt, which erodes one's financial well-being.

The Root Causes of Wealth Gap Inequality

Throughout generations, people of color in the US have faced significant barriers to homeownership due to discriminatory practices known as redlining. From 1934 to 1962, the Federal Housing Administration (FHA) implemented policies that systematically denied credit and insurance for mortgages to non-White individuals. This resulted in the exclusion of African American communities from homeownership opportunities. Under the FHA's redlining practices, mortgages were denied or made inaccessible for properties in and near African American neighborhoods. Meanwhile, the FHA subsidized the construction of suburban developments exclusively for White families, explicitly prohibiting the sale of homes to African Americans. This government-sanctioned segregation further perpetuated racial inequality by confining people of color to urban housing projects (Rothstein 2017).

These discriminatory policies created a lasting impact and contributed significantly to today's persistent racial wealth gap. The exclusion of people of color from homeownership opportunities denied them the ability to build equity and accumulate wealth through property ownership. We must confront these obstacles to address this systemic issue and create asset-building access.

Firstly, we need to address the discrimination and unconscious bias within the investment community. By promoting inclusivity and diversity within financial institutions, we can ensure that people of color have equal access to investment opportunities and financial resources. Secondly, we must address the inequitable access to the essential factors contributing to social, physical, and economic well-being. This includes providing culturally relevant and accessible financial literacy and personal finance education. Equipping individuals from marginalized communities with the necessary knowledge and tools can empower them to make informed financial decisions, save effectively, and participate in wealth-building activities. While achieving structural transformation takes time, we can close the racial wealth gap and foster a more equitable society by addressing these obstacles.

Why Not Invest?

Why aren't more people of color investing? Several reasons include fear, lack of savings, limited access to financial literacy, and insufficient disposable income. These barriers to investment stem from historical and structural discrimination that hinders wealth accumulation in marginalized communities. However, there are ways to overcome these challenges.

One solution is to provide investment opportunities tailored explicitly for Black or Latinx-led businesses. By offering investment products and resources that cater to the needs and aspirations of these communities, we can encourage greater participation in investment activities. Improving access to financial education is another crucial step. Investment education should be made more accessible through user-friendly platforms, available in multiple languages, and leveraging innovative technologies. To ensure individuals have the necessary knowledge and tools to navigate the investment landscape, we can empower them to make informed decisions about their financial future.

A personal example that highlights the importance of retirement savings is my brother, Domingo Rafael. Despite being a college graduate with a compassionate nature, he cannot fully retire at the age of sixty-nine. He did not prioritize saving in a private retirement plan such as a 401(k) but instead relied on government-assisted programs to meet his basic needs. For example, working as a maintenance or janitorial worker created a need for more access to employer-sponsored retirement benefits. He feared losing his hard-earned money and admits that not knowing about investments deterred him from saving for retirement. He said, "My trust in God sustains me." His situation underscores the significance of preparing for retirement.

I value my brother's perspective, which resonates with many people of color. It highlights the need to create improved financial literacy educational systems that serve individuals like Domingo. Our current systems need to adequately address the unique challenges that marginalized individuals face. To benefit future generations, it is essential to incorporate financial literacy, saving habits, credit management, and investment practices into early education. By instilling these skills from a young age, we can develop healthy financial habits, avoid predatory financial products, and build an effective relationship with money.

We must address the systemic barriers to investing and fostering a culture of financial empowerment. We can help individuals of color achieve greater financial security and build a more equitable society.

Solution for Asset-Building

Addressing the racial wealth gap and promoting asset-building is a crucial focus for Centro, as we provide entrepreneurship education and financial literacy training to the community.

People of color must have equal access to education, fair pay, financial services, and wealth-building opportunities. While Centro supported numerous entrepreneurs in establishing their businesses, we recognize many individuals can save but are hesitant to invest. They must be taught and trained about investing in assets such as retirement plans or homeownership.

To bridge this gap, Centro is developing a comprehensive asset-building program to assist the entrepreneurs we serve in saving and investing. We understand savings can gradually grow into investments, serving as a reliable strategy for retirement planning. By implementing an innovative, scalable model, we aim to create a robust saving-investment system that meets the specific needs of underserved communities.

The asset-building program by Centro encompasses the following steps:

1. Provide a financial literacy program focusing on saving and investing practices.
2. Develop culturally relevant methods for saving and investment education.
3. Establish access through a scalable technology-driven platform.
4. Collaborate with trusted, licensed financial advisors of color who can offer guidance on vetted investment options.

It is natural to build rapport with people who look similar to you. Having a financial advisor who shares similar life experiences and represents one's community fosters trust. Trust plays a significant role in personal finances and investment decisions, especially retirement planning. By partnering with trusted financial advisors (fiduciaries) of color, we aim to build that essential trust and guide individuals through saving and investing options, thus promoting asset-building.

Enhancing access to asset-building education will lead to wealth accumulation that remains within communities of color. According to studies by the NAACP, the average lifespan of a dollar is significantly shorter within Black communities compared to other communities. The average lifespan of the dollar is approximately twenty-eight days within Asian communities, nineteen days within Jewish communities, seventeen days within White communities—and just six hours within Black communities (Marshall 2020). We can bridge the wealth gap by addressing this disparity. While this challenge is complex, Centro believes in implementing scalable and impactful interventions to test our theory of change.

We can empower individuals with financial knowledge. Centro aims to fill the gaps and contribute to the equitable growth of underserved communities by providing access to trusted advisors and fostering financial literacy education and training for savings and investment.

Evaluate Your Financial Life

Leading Centro to support and empower entrepreneurs like my mother is my source of love. I am grateful for the valuable lessons she taught me about savings and investing, guiding my financial journey.

Before embarking on any new initiative, I encourage you to take a moment to evaluate your finances. A solid financial foundation allows you to channel your energy and focus on problem-solving and leadership. I underwent radical changes in my finances just before the onset of the COVID-19 pandemic, intending to realize my personal and financial goals.

My first step was to live below my means, ensuring I saved a significant portion of my income. Initially, this required making difficult choices and downsizing my lifestyle. I moved in with my brother, which helped me save money and reduce unnecessary expenses. While it represented a significant adjustment, it was the best decision I could have made, providing me with newfound financial security.

I strongly advise seeking assistance from financial advisors (fiduciaries) and coaches who can educate you on building wealth within your means. In my own experience, I learned about index investment funds, the power of compound interest, and various asset classes to consider for investment. Additionally, I recommend engaging with podcasts, audiobooks, and webinars led by reputable advisors on asset-building. It is also essential to prioritize building an emergency fund, eliminating debt, and saving for retirement.

As I witness my savings grow, my confidence grows alongside it. My mindset surrounding money changed positively as I cultivated a healthier relationship with it. Instead of allowing money to control me, I have taken control of my finances. Saving my hard-earned income brings me a sense of pride and accomplishment. If necessary, I'm also ready to help my family or friends in financial need.

Look to adopt these strategies and develop a positive psychology about money. Then you will improve your attitude regarding your finances and foster a healthy relationship with money. Remember, mastering money is within your reach, and you can achieve financial well-being with self-discipline.

Summary

In conclusion, starting small businesses can provide entrepreneurs with a stable source of income. However, it is crucial to consider whether entrepreneurs are also saving for emergencies and retirement amidst their focus on business growth.

While the initial years of business ownership are financially challenging, once businesses start generating profits, entrepreneurs must allocate a portion of their earnings to retirement savings. This ensures long-term financial security and stability.

Olga's story exemplifies the resourcefulness of entrepreneurs as she leveraged her skills and sought collaboration with her relatives to launch her business. This highlights the importance of finding creative solutions and partnerships when formal credit options are limited. She also kept in mind the importance of savings.

Saving and investing habits in the United States vary significantly across racial and ethnic groups, with significant wealth disparities. People of color face unique challenges when building wealth, with White families possessing significantly higher median wealth than Black and Hispanic families. To address these disparities, we must tackle discrimination and unconscious bias within the investment community. Promoting inclusivity and diversity in financial institutions ensures equal access to investment opportunities for people of color. Additionally, providing culturally relevant and accessible financial literacy education is essential—equipping individuals from marginalized communities with financial knowledge tools and empowering them to make informed decisions, save effectively, and participate in wealth-building activities.

By addressing these issues, we can create a more equitable society where entrepreneurs from all backgrounds have equal opportunities to build wealth and achieve financial independence.

Key Lessons

- *Building savings is essential to prepare for unforeseen circumstances.*
- *Adopting a lifestyle that allows you to live below your means is beneficial, aiming to save around 15 percent of your income.*
- *Saving serves as a foundation for long-term investments, particularly for retirement planning.*
- *Investing is crucial for asset-building and ultimately achieving financial independence.*
- *Developing new systems and structures that promote equal access to savings and investment opportunities is imperative.*

CONCLUSION

——◆◇◆——

I now pass the baton of leadership on to you, the new generation of social impact leaders. Armed with an arsenal of resources and opportunities, you stand on the precipice of immense community impact. Use this book as your compass, guiding you through the social change labyrinth and equipping you with the knowledge, inspiration, and tools to unleash your full potential and ignite lasting change within the communities you serve.

Together, let us sculpt a future where social impact knows no boundaries, equity and prosperity flourish, and the next generation of leaders fearlessly navigate uncharted waters, leaving indelible footprints on the sands of time.

Unlocking the potential of the next generation of social impact leaders, the torch is passed from generation to generation, each carrying the responsibility to drive change and improve communities. Today, I stand before you, fueled by a profound belief that the next generation of leaders will be better equipped and empowered to make an extraordinary difference. As you embark on this transformative journey, remember that even in the darkest moments, remarkable opportunities can emerge.

Cast your mind back to the beginning of 2009, when the weight of being laid off from my management consulting job bore heavily on my shoulders, and I found myself wandering through life's labyrinth. During these darkest hours, I experienced a profound transformation—a turning point that would shape the trajectory of my purpose. From despair, I emerged resolute and determined to serve others. Little did I know that the moment I lost my job would become a catalyst for the most significant turning point in my life—the moment I encountered Adela. Her unwavering faith in me shattered the barriers of self-doubt and ignited a flame within my soul.

Through my unwavering commitment to community impact, I have devoted nearly fourteen years to Centro, an organization that became the cornerstone of my personal growth and healing. As I reflect upon this transformative journey, excitement courses through my veins. I eagerly anticipate the next evolution of Centro and the boundless possibilities that lie on the horizon.

What fills my heart with hope is the belief that, within the next five to ten years, we have the potential to witness a seismic shift in the economic development system. In this era, systemic racism is dismantled, and access to capital, entrepreneurship education, financial literacy, and asset-building reach unprecedented heights. And in this era of transformative change, we harness the power of artificial intelligence (AI) to amplify our impact to help create thriving communities.

But let us not limit ourselves to isolated victories. Let us dare to dream of a comprehensive economic development system that weaves together a collaborative ecosystem, technological innovation, asset-building resources, and entrepreneurship education, transcending boundaries and closing the racial wealth gap forever.

A Bigger Idea

My vision is to create a socioeconomic community-based solution that offers equitable access to a national virtual hub of entrepreneurship development resources for low-to-moderate-income entrepreneurs in underserved communities.

Centro's future focus is to build a complete economic development system that can nurture new business ideas, business formation, growth, and maturity, creating asset-building to empower millions of entrepreneurs to achieve financial stability and economic mobility.

To achieve a more equitable society, tackling discrimination and unconscious bias within the investment community is necessary. Promoting inclusivity and diversity in financial institutions ensures equal access to investment opportunities and resources for people of color. Additionally, addressing the gaps in access to essential factors like financial literacy, business planning, and entrepreneurship education is crucial. By providing culturally relevant and accessible financial education, individuals from marginalized communities can make informed financial decisions and participate in wealth-building activities. While achieving structural transformation takes time, addressing these obstacles helps to close the racial wealth gap and create a more equitable society.

My priority is to foster community uniting and rebuilding systems for those discriminated against for their color, gender, and disabilities. I aim to serve and contribute to the transformative process of entrepreneurs and social impact leaders who want to realize their dreams of a better life for themselves, their families, and their community.

We can create better systems for economic inclusion and opportunity and establish lasting enterprises led by people of color that result from their creative force and labor of love. Then they can retire in their golden years with dignity and financial freedom and create generational wealth for their descendants.

Key Takeaways

In a world free from systemic, institutional, and interrelational racism, self-determination and thriving would be accessible to all. However, the current economic development system is plagued by injustice, bias, and discrimination, which hinders equal access and success. Creating new systems that promote equity and equal opportunities is crucial to address these challenges.

Entrepreneurship is a proven pathway to financial stability and asset-building, especially for people of color and women entrepreneurs. By supporting and empowering these individuals, we can usher in a new era of economic prosperity and dismantle the barriers of racism within our institutional systems.

Small business ownership increases household income, promotes financial independence, and provides economic mobility. Unfortunately, discrimination and systemic racism still exist within financial institutions, creating barriers for aspiring entrepreneurs. To overcome these challenges, it is essential to uncover the issues surrounding access to capital and the infrastructure of the small business development ecosystem.

Nonprofit microenterprise development organizations like Centro are vital in addressing these challenges. They tailor their programs to meet the specific needs of low-income entrepreneurs that produce a significant positive impact on the entrepreneurs.

Creating meaningful change requires clear and concise mission and vision statements. Organizations with lengthy mission statements risk losing focus and effectiveness. As a leader, it is important to access resources, develop a capable staff, and serve as a force for positive societal change. Leaders can drive progress and promote equity by implementing new system changes that include the underserved. Personal and shared values are the glue that keeps the team engaged in the mission and vision. Embracing transformation is part of the social change process as it involves shedding old habits and insecurities to reach higher levels of self-awareness and skill.

Thorough research is essential to understand the scope of a social problem and develop practical solutions. Designing a pilot program allows for testing and gaining insights into the solution's viability. Credibility and trust are crucial when seeking funds and support for a social impact venture. A comprehensive business plan, backed by research and a compelling case study, demonstrates the viability and potential success of the social impact organization. Understanding one's unique qualifications to address the problem and identifying potential gaps or challenges in the planning process are vital for overcoming obstacles and ensuring the smooth execution of the business idea.

Fundraising is a key skill for starting a charitable organization or social enterprise. This skill can be learned through training and practice. Nonprofit volunteers often have firsthand experience witnessing a program's tangible impact on the communities they serve, which can provide valuable experience for fundraising. Determining the appropriate amount of funding to ask for is an important step before seeking support for a social impact organization.

Embarking on starting a social impact organization requires psychological preparation, resilience, and readiness to navigate self-sacrifice. When implementing social intervention programs, it is crucial to consider the diverse characteristics of the beneficiaries, such as age, educational attainment, socioeconomics, and gender. Determining the components of the intervention and measuring the results are essential for understanding the long-term impact.

For social interventions to be taken seriously by funders, other credible sources must document and observe the social issue. Credibility is necessary to gain the trust of funders, investors, and followers. Keep accurate measurements and report the results of the intervention so you understand the short- and long-term effects of the desired impact.

Innovation involves a series of successes and failures. Be willing to try new approaches, even if they seem unconventional. Curiosity and a love of learning can lead to innovative solutions. Challenging existing assumptions and paradigms is necessary to create change and solve social problems effectively.

Becoming an effective nonprofit leader requires personal growth, continuous learning, and the development of essential skills. Leaders can navigate the complexities of leading mission-focused and impactful community organizations by cultivating empathy, logical thinking, effective communication, high standards, and inner strength.

Effective team building involves self-assessment, understanding organizational needs, and careful selection and recruitment processes. Embracing diversity and inclusivity can lead to successful teams. Investing in innovation, technology, talent, and professional development is crucial for nonprofit and social enterprise organizations to survive and thrive in their mission to create lasting impact and sustainability.

An effective asset-building program includes providing financial literacy, developing culturally relevant methods, and establishing access through scalable technology-driven platforms. The goal at Centro is to see thriving entrepreneurs create wealth that uplifts their lives and strengthens their communities.

By embracing these principles and approaches, nonprofit and community impact leaders can create meaningful change, address social problems, and work toward a more equitable and prosperous society.

Join the Movement for Equity and Social Change!

We invite you to participate in a transformative movement to create a more equitable and just society for all. Together, we can break down the barriers of systemic racism, discrimination, and inequality that persist in our communities and institutions. It's time to take action and drive meaningful change.

Whether you're an entrepreneur, a community leader, a philanthropist, or an advocate for social justice, your voice and actions matter. Here's how you can get involved:

1. *Educate Yourself:* Take the time to learn about the root causes of systemic racism, social injustice, and inequality. Engage in critical conversations, read insightful literature, and seek diverse perspectives. Knowledge is power; understanding the issues is the first step to creating lasting change.
2. *Support Minority-Owned Businesses:* By consciously supporting minority-owned businesses, you can contribute to economic empowerment and help bridge the wealth gap. Seek out and patronize businesses owned by people of color, women entrepreneurs, and other marginalized groups. Together, we can create a thriving ecosystem that uplifts underrepresented voices.

3. *Advocate for Policy Change:* Use your voice to advocate for policies that promote equality, justice, and opportunity for all. Write to your representatives, participate in local community meetings, and support organizations working to reform policy. We can shape a more inclusive future by amplifying the voices of those who have been marginalized.

4. *Volunteer and Engage:* Get involved in grassroots organizations, nonprofits, and initiatives dedicated to social change. Whether it's mentoring aspiring entrepreneurs, organizing community events, or offering your skills and expertise, your contributions can have a meaningful impact. We can build a strong support network and empower individuals and communities.

5. *Donate and Invest:* Financial contributions are vital to fueling the work of organizations fighting for equity and social justice. Consider donating to nonprofits focusing on racial and social equity or investing in impact-driven ventures prioritizing positive change. Financial support can create opportunities, break down barriers, and empower individuals and communities.

6. *Be an Ally:* Listen, learn, and empathize with those who have experienced discrimination and marginalization. Stand up against racism, sexism, and all forms of injustice. Use your privilege to amplify marginalized voices and actively work to dismantle systems of oppression.

We can create a future where equal access to opportunities, resources, and success is embraced. Join us in this collective journey to a more equitable and just society. Take action today and be the catalyst for positive change.

ACKNOWLEDGMENTS

This book was a labor of love, fueled by a deep belief in the potential of the next generation of social impact leaders. Reflecting on the journey that led me to this point, I am humbled by the incredible individuals who have influenced and supported me.

I want to begin by expressing my sincere gratitude to Adela. When I hit rock bottom and lost my sense of direction, her unwavering faith in me ignited a spark of hope. Adela, you changed the course of my life, and I will forever be grateful for your belief in my potential.

To the Centro team, thank you for embracing me as a member of this incredible organization. For almost fourteen years, I have witnessed the transformative power of your work. Your dedication, passion, and unwavering commitment to social impact have inspired me every step of the way.

I would also like to acknowledge the individuals who have guided and shaped my understanding of community impact and economic development. Your wisdom, insights, and willingness to share your knowledge were invaluable. Together, we are laying the foundation for a brighter future and creating a more inclusive and equitable economic system.

Thank you to my family and friends for your unwavering support, love, and encouragement. Your belief in my abilities and constant motivation was the driving force behind my journey. I am truly blessed to have you by my side.

I am deeply grateful to my work's readers, editors, and thought partners who supported my ideas and shared their valuable feedback. Your engagement and enthusiasm have inspired me to continue pushing the boundaries of what is possible and to strive for greater impact.

Lastly, I want to extend my heartfelt appreciation to the broader community of change-makers and social entrepreneurs. Your relentless pursuit of social justice, equity, and positive change inspires us all. Together, we can create a future where systemic racism is dismantled, and resources are accessible to all.

As we embark on this journey to a comprehensive economic development system, I am excited about the possibilities. We can bring about real change in underserved communities with collaborative ecosystems, technological innovation, and a commitment to closing the racial wealth gap.

To the next generation of social impact leaders, this book is dedicated to you. May it serve as a roadmap, providing you with the tools, resources, and inspiration needed to create lasting change in the communities you serve. Together, we can build a brighter and more equitable future for all.

To everyone who played a part, big or small, in the creation of this book, I am truly grateful. Your support and contributions have made this endeavor possible, and I am honored to have you by my side.

Editors

Anna Noriega

Asia McDougall

Daniel John (DJ) Healy

Domingo Rafael Noriega

Gina Champagne

George Thorne

Luisa Fernanda Chinchilla

Mary Ann Tate

Pavita Singh

Ruth Kim

Scott Aronowitz

Tom Horracks

Centro Team

Carlo Arellano

Claudia Saez de Gordoa

Damanbir Singh

Estefania Cardona

Lesly Arellano

Naldo Peliks

Simone Harvey

Vernisha Willams

Verónica Gutiérrez

Presale Supporters

Adrian Medina

Alejandra Ayala

Alexandre Applefield

Alice Miller

Andrea Gonzalez Duarte

Anne Vrooman

Anir Chakravorty

Anita Dharapuram

Baijanta Bharali

Bernadette Marjanovic

Bob Friedman

Camila Vega Freedman

Carmen Guerrero

Carly Perera

Celina Pena

Cindy Eggleton

Christine Doerr

Claudia Damiani

Claudia Rivas

Claudia Viek

Curtis Widdoes

Daniel Galindo

Damanbir Singh
Daphne Jefferson
Darius Mahajer
David Chavez
David Green
David Onek
David Meader
Denise Morones
Diana Zepeda
Dion Reyes Quiocho
Dipak Javiya
Domingo R. Noriega
Dmitriy Lyan
Elena Widdoes
Emile Pilafidis
Eric Koester
Felicia Pierson
Felix Fan
George Clapsis
Glenn Fishler
Heward Jue
Hope Harley
Iryna Oreshkova
Jacob Gelfand
Jane Colacicco
Janine Firpo
Jeanne Wardford
Jennifer Cisneros
Jennifer Madden
Joel Ojeda Ramírez
John Peters
Joseph Martin

Jovan Hicks
Joyce Windross
Julia Conant
Julie Abrams
Julie Schmidlen
Julius Robinson
Justin Simpson
Karen Carter
Kathryn Svobodny
Kelley Stupfel Conway
Kerwin Charles
Kwan Kong
Leticia Landa
Liane Lanterman
Lliana Pérez
Lisa Margulies
Liz Fanning
Lorena Grajeda
Lorinda Ruddiman
Madelyn Mackie
Madel Leal
Marcos González
Marc Rand
Maren Colon
Marie Millares
Martin Guerrero
Manahari Hansel
Matthew Spiegel
Melissa Gallegos
Melissa Proctor
Michael Conant
Michael Berger

Michael Gutiérrez
Michael Wray
Miguel Iraola
Mimi Hernández
Mónica Limas
Monique Hector
Ngozi Okaro
Oscar A. Noriega
Oliver Scott
Orlando Harris
Paola Vergara
Paula Bryan
Preeti Narang
Raminder Somal
Ramona Bowen
Richard Park
Rodolfo Sachun
Rolando Noriega
Rosa Guerrero Contreras

Ruth Kim
Saundra Hodges
Sean Chon
Sephora Pierre Louis
Susan Howard
Sheetal Kapani
Stella Carakasi
Steven Hoskinson
Steven White
Tania Han
Tara Davos
Topher Wilkins
Travis Wilkins
Vera Moore
Vernisha Williams
Vijay Sathe
William Vetten
Yasnay Montalvo
Yolanda Robinson

Special Support
Jay Wang
Patricia Alanya Rojas

APPENDIX

Introduction

University of Southern California. 2021. "How to Explain Structural, Institutional and Systemic Racism." *The MSW@USC Blog* (Blog). October 26, 2021. https://msw.usc.edu/mswusc-blog/how-to-explain-structural-institutional-and-systemic-racism/.

Chapter 1

Arraiz, Irani, María Paula Gerardino, Jimena Serrano, Patricia Yañez-Pagans. 2022. "Uncovering the Hidden Cost of Gender Biases in Lending to Women." IDB Invest. Accessed May 20, 2023. https://idbinvest.org/en/blog/gender/uncovering-hidden-cost-gender-biases-lending-women

Buttle, Rhett. 2021. "Empowering Women Entrepreneurs of Color a Conversation with Ayris T. Scales, CEO of Walker's Legacy Foundation." *Forbes.* May 25, 2021. https://www.forbes.com/sites/rhettbuttle/2021/05/25/empowering-women-entrepreneurs-of-color-a-conversation-with-ayris-t-scales-ceo-of-walkers-legacy-foundation/.

Costa, Daniel. 2022. "Entrepreneurship." *Encyclopaedia Britannica* s.v. Accessed November 15, 2022. https://www.britannica.com/topic/entrepreneurship.

George, Alice. 2019. "How Business Executive Madam C. J. Walker Became a Powerful Influencer of the Early 20th Century." *Smithsonian Magazine*. March 21, 2019. https://www.smithsonianmag.com/smithsonian-institution/how-business-executive-madam-c-j-walker-became-powerful-influencer-early-20th-century-180971628/.

Gomez-Aguinaga, Barbara. 2022. "State of Latino Entrepreneurship Report." Stanford University. Accessed November 21, 2022. https://www.gsb.stanford.edu/sites/default/files/publication/pdfs/state-latino-entrepreneurship-2022.pdf.

Hernandez Kent, Ana, and David F. Perkis. 2022. "Page One Economics, Examining Racial Wealth Inequality." March 2022. ResearchStLouis.org. https://files.stlouisfed.org/files/htdocs/publications/page1-econ/2022/03/01/examining-racial-wealth-inequality_SE.pdf.

Kelley, Donna, Mahdi Majbouri, and Angela Randolph. 2021. "Black Women Are More Likely to Start a Business than White Men." *Harvard Business Review*. Accessed October 15, 2022. https://hbr.org/2021/05/black-women-are-more-likely-to-start-a-business-than-white-men.

Klein, Joyce, and Carol Wayman. 2008. "Encouraging Entrepreneurship, A Microenterprise Development Policy Agenda." Aspen Institute. https://www.frbsf.org/community-develop-

ment/wp-content/uploads/sites/3/klein_wayman_engaging_
entrepreneurship.pdf.

Marin Health and Human Services. 2021. "Equity vs. Equality: What's the Difference?" Accessed Dec 10, 2021. www.
marinhhs.org/sites/default/files/boards/general/equality_v._
equity_04_05_2021.pdf.

McShane, Kathleen. 2019. "Mentoring: The Missing Link to Small
Business Growth and Survival." *Small Business Administration*
(Blog). February 4, 2019. https://www.sba.gov/blog/mentoring-missing-link-small-business-growth-survival.

San Diego Foundation. 2022. "What Is Social Justice?" September
24, 2022. https://www.sdfoundation.org/news-events/sdf-news/
what-is-social-justice/.

Smith, Tyler. 2023. "Gender Bias in Bank Lending." American Economic Association. Accessed on May 20, 2023. https://www.
aeaweb.org/research/discriminatory-lending-lab-turkey

Stephenson, Kristen. 2021. "First Self-Made Millionairess."
Guinness World Records. February 16, 2021. https://www.
guinnessworldrecords.com/world-records/first-self-made-millionairess?fb_comment_id=683116778469956_160097837001
7121.

The Annie E. Casey Foundation. 2020. "Equity vs. Equality and
Other Racial Justice Definitions." *The Annie E. Casey Foundation* (Blog). August 24, 2020. www.aecf.org/blog/racial-justice-definitions.

Chapter 2

Centro Community Partners. 2023. "Centro Community Partners Overview" Accessed April 30, 2023. https://www.centrocommunity.org/overview.

Commerce Institute. 2023. "What Percentage of Small Businesses Fail Each Year? Fewer Than You Think." Accessed on May 12, 2023. https://www.commerceinstitute.com/business-failure-rate/#:~:text=Fewer%20Than%20You%20Think.,survive%20at%20least%20fifteen%20years.

Klein, Joyce, and Carol Wayman. 2008. "Encouraging Entrepreneurship, A Microenterprise Development Policy Agenda." Aspen Institute. https://www.frbsf.org/community-development/wp-content/uploads/sites/3/klein_wayman_engaging_entrepreneurship.pdf.

PayScale. 2023. "Average Small Business Owner Salary." PayScale.com. Accessed May 15, 2023. https://www.payscale.com/research/US/Job=Small_Business_Owner/Salary.

The Urban Institute. 2008. "Key Findings from the Evaluation of the Small Business Administration's Loan and Investment Programs." Accessed by May 15, 2023. https://www.urban.org/sites/default/files/publication/31426/411602-Key-Findings-from-the-Evaluation-of-the-Small-Business-Administration-s-Loan-and-Investment-Programs.PDF.

U.S. Census Bureau. 2018. "Nonemployer Statistics by Demographics." Annual Business Survey. Accessed on May 14, 2023. https://www.census.gov/programs-surveys/abs.html.

Chapter 3

Bart, Christopher, and Mark C. Baetz. 1998. "The Relationship between Mission Statements and Firm Performance: An Exploratory Study." *Journal of Management Studies* 35, no. 3 (November): 823–853. https://doi.org/10.1111/1467-6486.00121.

Bart, Christopher, and Mark C. Baetz. 1998. "The Relationship Between Mission Statements and Firm Performance: An Exploratory Study." *Journal of Management Studies* 35 no. 6 (July): 823-853. https://doi.org/10.1111/1467-6486.00121.

Bart, Christopher, Nick Bontis, and Simon Taggar. 2001. "A Model of the Impact of Mission Statements on Firm Performance." *Management Decision* 39, no. 1 (February): 19–35.

Chapter 5

Klein, Joyce, and Carol Wayman. 2008. "Encouraging Entrepreneurship, A Microenterprise Development Policy Agenda." Aspen Institute. https://www.frbsf.org/community-development/wp-content/uploads/sites/3/klein_wayman_engaging_entrepreneurship.pdf.

Dorsey, Cheryl, Jeff Bradach, and Peter Kim. 2020. "Racial Equity and Philanthropy: Disparities in Funding for Leaders of Color Leave Impact on the Table." The Bridgespan Group. May 4, 2020. https://www.bridgespan.org/insights/disparities-non-profit-funding-for-leaders-of-color.

Lambert, Melanie. 2022. "6 Reasons You Shouldn't Ask for a Grant Writer's Success Rate." June 28, 2023. Just Write Grants. Accessed May 17, 2023. https://www.justwritegrants.com/post/successrate#.

Professional Grant Writer. 2021. *What Is a Good Grant Writing Success Rate?* (Blog). December 14, 2021. https://www.professionalgrantwriter.org/learn-rejected-grant-proposal.

Chapter 6

American Express. 2019. "The 2019 State of Women-Owned Businesses Report." Accessed June 10, 2022. https://ventureneer.com/wp-content/uploads/2019/10/Final-2019-state-of-women-owned-businesses-report.pdf.

Barr, Michael. 2015. "Minority and Women Entrepreneurs: Building Capital, Networks, and Skills." The Hamilton Project. https://www.brookings.edu/wp-content/uploads/2016/07/minority_women_entrepreneurs_building_skills_barr.pdf.

Cantwell, Maria. 2014. "21st Century Barriers to Women's Entrepreneurship Majority Report of the U.S. Senate Committee on Small Business and Entrepreneurship." Accessed June 10, 2022. https://www.sbc.senate.gov/public/_cache/files/3/f/3f954386-f16b-48d2-86ad-698a75e33cc4/F74C-2CA266014842F8A3D86C3AB619BA.21st-century-barriers-to-women-s-entrepreneurship-revised-ed.-v.1.pdf.

Centro Community Partners. 2022. "Centro Community Partners Impact Report." Accessed April 30, 2023. https://static1.squarespace.com/static/55fb5f60e4b0766e57f5d313/t/6390c-59c549d5b29b102ca37/1670432193053/Centro+Community+Partners+Impact+Report+-+Sept+2022.pdf.

Fund Against Child Labour. 2018. "Theory of Change Guidelines." Fund Against Child Labour. Accessed August 12, 2022.

https://english.rvo.nl/sites/default/files/2018/11/FBK_theory_of_change_guidelines_0.pdf.

Net Promoter System. 2023. "History of Net Promoter." Net Promoter System. Accessed June 10, 2022. https://www.netpromotersystem.com/about/history-of-net-promoter/.

Poverty Action. 2016. "Goldilocks Deep Dive Guiding Your Program to Build Theory of Change." Poverty Action.org. Accessed August 12, 2022. https://poverty-action.org/sites/default/files/publications/Goldilocks-Deep-Dive-Guiding-Your-Program-to-Build-Theory-of-Change_2.pdf.

Chapter 7

Aspen Institute. 2014. "U.S. Microenterprise Census Highlights." Accessed November 12, 2022. https://www.aspeninstitute.org/wp-content/uploads/2017/04/CensusHighlightsFY2014.pdf.

Landry, Lauren. 2020. "What Is Human-Centered Design?" Harvard Business School. Accessed May 15, 2023. https://online.hbs.edu/blog/post/what-is-human-centered-design.

Lawson, Stephen. 2010. "2010 Called Breakthrough Year for Mobile Apps." Computerworld. Accessed January 15, 2022. https://www.computerworld.com/article/2516719/2010-called-breakthrough-year-for-mobile-apps.html.

ProductPlan. 2023. "What Is a Minimum Viable Product?" Accessed May 20, 2023. https://www.productplan.com/glossary/minimum-viable-product/.

Chapter 8

Center for American Progress. 2020. "States Ranked by Overall Poverty Rate 2020." Talk Poverty. Accessed January 10, 2023. https://talkpoverty.org/poverty.html.

Centro Community Partners. 2022. "Centro Community Partners Overview." Accessed April 30, 2023. https://www.centrocommunity.org/overview.

Centro Community Partners. 2022. "Centro Community Partners Impact Report." Accessed April 30, 2023. https://static1.squarespace.com/static/55fb5f60e4b0766e57f5d313/t/6390c-59c549d5b29b102ca37/1670432193053/Centro+Community+Partners+Impact+Report+-+Sept+2022.pdf.

U.S. Census Bureau. 2022. "Poverty in the United States: 2021." Census.gov. Accessed January 11, 2023. https://www.census.gov/library/publications/2022/demo/p60-277.html.

Chapter 9

Hesselbein, Frances. 2002. *Hesselbein on Leadership.* San Francisco: Jossey-Bass

Chapter 10

Drucker, Peter. 1973. *Management: Tasks, Responsibilities, and Practices.* New York: Harper Press.

IPM Advancement. 2023. "Nonprofit Staff Retention, Are Higher Salaries Really the Answer." IPM Advancement. Accessed July 10, 2022. https://www.ipmadvancement.com/blog/nonprofit-staff-retention-are-higher-salaries-really-the-answer#.

Salamon, Lester, and Chelsea Newhouse. 2020. "2020 Nonprofit Employment Report." Johns Hopkins Center for Civil Society Studies. Accessed July 10, 2022. http://ccss.jhu.edu/wp-content/uploads/downloads/2020/06/2020-Nonprofit-Employment-Report_FINAL_6.2020.pdf.

U.S. Bureau of Labor Statistics. 2020. "Median Tenure with Current Employer Was 4.1 Years in January 2020." The Economic Daily. September 29, 2020. https://www.bls.gov/opub/ted/2020/median-tenure-with-current-employer-was-4-point-1-years-in-january-2020.htm.

Chapter 11

McRae, Greg, EA. 2022. *Top 5 Reasons Why Nonprofits Fail* (Blog). CEO's Blog. October 21, 2022. Foundation Group. https://www.501c3.org/top-5-reasons-why-nonprofits-fail/#.

Morris, George, Dylan Roberts, John MacIntosh, and Adrian Bordone. 2018. "The Financial Health of the United States Nonprofit Sector." Oliver Wyman and GuideStar, Marsh & McLennan Companies. January 2018. https://www.issuelab.org/resources/38539/38539.pdf.

NCCS Team. 2020. "The Nonprofit Sector in Brief." National Center on Charitable Statistics. June 18, 2020. https://nccs.urban.org/project/nonprofit-sector-brief.

Chapter 12

Caporal, Jack and Lyle Daly. 2023. "Study: Race and Personal Finance in America." The Motley Fool Ascent. Accessed January 10, 2023. https://www.fool.com/the-ascent/research/study-race-personal-finance-america/#.

Bhutta, Neil, Andrew C. Chang, Lisa J. Dettling, and Joanne W. Hsu. 2020. "Disparities in Wealth by Race and Ethnicity in the 2019 Survey of Consumer Finances." Board of Governors of U.S. Federal Reserve. September 28, 2020. Accessed May 15, 2023. https://www.federalreserve.gov/econres/notes/feds-notes/disparities-in-wealth-by-race-and-ethnicity-in-the-2019-survey-of-consumer-finances-20200928.html.

Dettling, Lisa, Joanne Hsu, Lindsay Jacobs, Kevin B. Moore, and Jeffrey P. Thompson. 2017. "Recent Trends in Wealth-Holding by Race and Ethnicity: Evidence from the Survey of Consumer Finances." Board of Governors of U.S. Federal Reserve. September 27, 2017. https://www.federalreserve.gov/econres/notes/feds-notes/recent-trends-in-wealth-holding-by-race-and-ethnicity-evidence-from-the-survey-of-consumer-finances-20170927.html.

Marshall, Kamryn. 2020. "The Black Dollar Doesn't Circulate Like It Should." The Famuan. October 1, 2020. http://www.thefamuanonline.com/2020/10/01/the-black-dollar-doesnt-circulate-like-it-should/.

Rothstein, Richard. 2017. *The Color of Law: A Forgotten History of How Our Government Segregated America.* New York: Liveright Publishing Corporation.

Routley, Nick. 2019. "How the Composition of Wealth Differs, from the Middle Class to the Top 1%." Visual Capitalist. May 18, 2019. https://www.visualcapitalist.com/composition-of-wealth/.

U.S. Bureau of Economic Analysis. 2023. "Personal Savings Rate." Federal Reserve Economic Data. April 23, 2023. https://fred.stlouisfed.org/series/PSAVERT.